SHE WHO WALKS
ALONE . . . WITH ONE

SHE WHO WALKS
ALONE . . . WITH ONE

Along your own journey
always Remember-
you are NEVER alone!
Shaley x

Shalisa Anthony

Library of Congress Control Number: 2012905917
ISBN: Hardcover   978-1-4691-9355-7
                Softcover   978-1-4691-9354-0
                Ebook   978-1-4691-9356-4

To order additional copies of this book, contact:
Xlibris Corporation
0-800-644-6988
www.xlibrispublishing.co.uk
Orders@xlibrispublishing.co.uk
303927

CONTENTS

ACKNOWLEDGEMENTS

Who can I thank but the One Who took me from my mother's womb, carried me through life and has now set my feet on a firm foundation? Who gets the praise for ordering and setting my steps thus far? None other but He Who walks with me still!

There's a special heartbeat for my Mum—my journey starting point—for living the true meaning of love, grace and mercy. Especial thanks to my Sister Donna Brown and friend Alison Agard for walking with me in my dark times and for allowing God to shine through you to light my way—and also to Molly Moyo for giving me the final push!

FOREWORDS

Hi Shalisa,

. . . When you asked me to edit your book I was not prepared for what would happen in terms of the mental rollercoaster that would ensue. I confess and apologise as my first reading of the book not only captivated but overwhelmed me immensely—I could/did not edit it. The book spoke to me and put me in a position that I have never been in before. I had to confront my own fears, secrets and feelings known and unknown which began to unravel all at once. I was not prepared for this. However, its subliminal captivating elements kept me entranced suffice enough to soothe and allow healing where needed. Indeed at some points I did not want to continue. This book is awesome and the potential inexhaustible. I chuckled to myself, laughed uncouthly and even cried. May God truly continue to bind you up in the bundle of the living; this key (your book) will open the door to freedom for many women (no matter how intact they claim to be). God bless and prosper your path for this sacrifice. With sincere love **"C"**

Shalisa is an ordinary church gal, but one of the brave few who expose her past for women to have a better future. Shalisa takes you through her life from the comforts of home and mum to shady characters . . . men, looking for just one thing. Shalisa dips in and out of her past to reveal her triumphs, mistakes, and madness with a unique sense of humour but always with a lesson learned. This book will take you through her epic journey of self discovery. Meet her friends and acquaintances as she opens door after door of opportunity and disappointment. Open this book and you are bound to find yourself on one of the pages. Rarely can you get this from the pulpit, a must read for every woman (and man) struggling to find who they are. **Marvyn Bramble**

This book is beautifully crafted and tailor-made for the broken hearted woman. Shalisa Anthony has skilfully and insightfully shown us a path to healing by uncovering her most intimate secrets and revealing the scars of her yesterday. With her unique comic flare, she opens door after door to the hidden chambers of her painful past and allows us a sneak peek into the complexities of the female mind. As she walks us through the pages of her broken life, we see the hands of a merciful God cutting deep into the heart of her emotions and carefully removing every trace of damaged and scarred tissue. With the precision of a neurosurgeon, He implants His words of life and empowers her to succeed. Shalisa Anthony encourages us to celebrate our womanhood in spite of it all, to "Walk Alone" with God and to trust in Him to reshape our destiny. I thoroughly enjoyed it!! **Rev. Jasmine Williams, PJW Ministries.**

CHAPTER OVERVIEW . . .

Overview:

Everyone, every woman has a story to tell, but few are willing to relive it much less have the courage to tell it. It's painful to watch yourself from your now enlightened place, do and say things you would never do now. It is hard for the swan to ever imagine the ugly duckling she knew so well, was once her—but it's true! It is hard to imagine how the sharing of a few of your life experiences can help heal a fellow traveller's hurt, can soothe a lonely hurt and comfort a tender soul. "SWWA . . . WO" is the sharing of my life journey as I traversed the pot holes of low self esteem and relational and emotional road works and many other issues we as women face along our own (and collective) life journeys. It is not a walk in the park but a look at a sista's journey from the shadows into the light—for when I thought it was all over, when I thought I was a dead-end, when I thought I was truly alone . . . I didn't know He was with me all along . . .

Chapter 1: Introduction

No drugs, sex or rock 'n' roll but a 2-part introduction illustrating how life sends many chances for us to restart our life's journey and continue our walk. It outlines the scene of a life journey to date by an "ordinary woman with an extraordinary dream" who dared to move beyond the "mundane and mediocre".

Chapter 2: Precious Moments

It's amazing how our past reflects where we are whilst simultaneously showing glimpses of where and what we could be. "Precious Moments" is a literary snapshot of childhood memories steeped in the exotic flavourings of the Caribbean with a generous sprinkling of love, laughter and food! It is also the bittersweet memories of wrong turns, dead-ends and road blocks . . . and a looking for love in all the wrong places.

Chapter 3: Sandwich Generation—Open Top Filling!

When you realise your life journey is not mapped out according to societal norms, it can be a hard and bitter pill to swallow. Although part of the "sandwich generation" by definition, this is specifically for those women who have to juggle care responsibilities for family at both ends of the spectrum—alone. This is their heart cry.

Chapter 4: Carnal Carnival

Oh, the bittersweet memory of your first love, the pain of losing it and finding you've embarked on a course you never realised would take you so far and for so long. "Carnal Carnival" explores some of the internal and external "push-pull" factors which you might recognise as having led you to your present place. It's a painful but necessary journey everyone needs to relive in order to get back on track . . .

Chapter 5: Ol' Chocolate

What do you do when your search for a father's love finds you walking away from the Ultimate Father . . . into the arms of a poor imitation? This chapter is a testimony to the truth of the title "She who Walks Alone . . . with One".

Chapter 6: The Move

Moving from one place to another and transitioning from one phase of one's journey to another, is not as smooth and as easy as it looks on TV makeover programmes. "The Move" is a humorous look at how relocation almost caused a dislocation in order to be in the right location and the reader is sure to find a truth behind the tears and purpose behind the pain.

Chapter 7: Shhh, Don't Tell

On any long trip, we eagerly look out for those signs offering food and respite at the next motorway café, so we can stop and take a much needed break. "Shhh, Don't Tell" is that break as the reader gets to meet and hear the experiences from other journey travellers. The compilation of true life stories and scenarios in this chapter reaches out to all women—for their journey experiences could well help you along your own path.

Chapter 8: Sista to Sista

This chapter captures a heart-to-heart moment with a sista, illustrating the need for us to carry one another's burdens in the sharing of how we overcame. "Sista-to-Sista" helps us realise the mistakes, slip ups and stumblings we made on our walk, can be a stepping stone for someone behind us, on their own life journey.

Chapter 9: My Journey Jewels

There is an old saying: "How can two walk together unless they be agreed?" Although such wisdom is often used when considering that "special someone", it is also relevant for those who you choose—or who life chooses—to walk with you. "My Journey Jewels" is in recognition of those whose extra sparkles and glistening shimmers have been a guiding light in my midnight walks of despair, low self-esteem and depression—and reminder for all to cherish their own "journey jewels".

Chapter 10: There But for Grace (go I)

Love, betrayal and finally grace and restoration are the main ingredients of this chapter. A realisation that one more day, one more step, one more look, one more touch could have placed us in a worse situation, if it wasn't for Someone Unseen, Unknown—but Ever-loving—walking with, watching over and willing you to make it. I believe this will resonate with many a reader and cause them to recognise in the midst of it all, Grace was with them.

Chapter 11: Pandora's Box

Just when you thought you'd done and seen it all; when you congratulate yourself on having clocked up many a-mile on your walk thus far, you got sidetracked! It was all too much to leave behind; you just HAD to open it . . . and like a game of "snakes and ladders", you've found yourself right at the bottom again . . . In this timely reminder not to open the box, always remember—all is not lost . . .

Chapter 12: Time to Get Back Up Again

Congratulations! You've made it this far! You're an experienced runner! You've seen, jumped and cleared all stumbling blocks—but ouch! What do you do when you've taken a fall? Your foot just clipped the last hurdle and, surely, you should have known better by now! "Time to Get Back Up Again", although the last chapter is a timely reminder that your journey is far from over—and points you to the One Who is ever by your side . . .

CHAPTER 1

Introduction

"Don't you know who I am!? Don't you know that the
God I serve, Jehovah Jireh, Jehovah Shammah, Jehovah
Shalom is with me and will provide for me"

Shalisa's dream, 5th April 2009

It begins . . . NOW!

It was a word that got me to finally pick up the pen and write this story, *my story,* which has been growing in me for all this time. From the faint fluttering of a newly conceived embryo to the rapid heartbeat of a ready-to-come forth baby, it has been in the womb of my very soul, just waiting for a sign, for the "quickening", to come.

Some 4-5 years ago, I shared my vision about birthing this dream with DD, my spirit sister. When she shared how she'd dreamt I'd actually gotten around to finishing the book, I recognised her dream to be my first birth signal. She then told me I needed to write it, as a "matter of urgency", I remember smiling and saying, "uh huh . . . hmm . . . yes, yes, okay DD!", as I quickly sought to change the subject, because giving birth to a dream can't be rushed can it; it will come in its own time. Don't get me wrong; over the years I've been aware of a tugging and a pulling towards the need to birth this, but there was always something, someone or a "situation" somewhere, along with a myriad of valid excuses, which would conveniently step up and present yet another reason why not now, not today. At those times, I'd think about it but did not seem to have the wherewithal to actually take it forward and yes, I began to doubt if it would ever happen. Little did I know the dream was not dead but silently growing and developing in the quietness and the darkness of life's circumstances and situations.

However, it was my work friend and prayer sister, MM, who caused the waters to break. One day at work, she said she had a "Word" for me (note: capital "W"!). While watching TV one Sunday, God told her to tell me that "I have anointed Shalisa to write, that is her anointing. She is to write for that is what I have anointed her to do". Now MM, being very obedient to deliver the message, eagerly waited for the right moment—which was when we were in the lift at work! She gleefully turned to me and said "Shalisa, remember the word I said I had for you?" "Yesss" (I was very cagey and wide-eyed at the time). "Well, Shalisa, you *have* to write! The Lord said you have to write and that He has anointed you to do so!" My initial response was one of panic and I wanted to run but guess what? It's very hard to try running out of a moving lift! Well, after she delivered the word, the dam burst and my waters started to flow, slow and steady at first, but, wow, I could feel it beginning to trickle slowly out before the full flow came. So, dear reader, you have been warned!

Please forgive me if, in the midst of my bringing forth, you hear my labour pains, cries and groans. Sorry if I grab your hand and squeeze it a little too tightly for comfort. Do pardon me, if you hear or see things, private, intimate issues which are usually best left unsaid or hidden from view, but you have to understand that giving birth and bringing forth will do expose your vulnerabilities and nakedness. It sure ain't pretty but is necessary for your baby, your vision, your dream, to be born. So treat this well and hold it gently, because this baby sure does look like me ~ because it IS me!

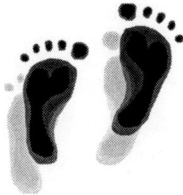

Welcome to "She Who Walks Alone . . . with One!"

My story is an ordinary woman's journey of simply "just keeping on". I did not have a magic wand, a crystal ball or a mystical moment. My life journey (thus far!) is not one of drugs, sex and rock and roll, so apologies to those looking for titillation and "kiss and tell" stories. No, this is my chance to tell my story to encourage the "ordinary" woman with an extraordinary dream, to know and recognise there is more to her beyond the mundane and mediocrity of her everyday life. In my journey thus far, I am amazed at the person who walks alongside me, understands, loves and encourages me, even when I really don't think I am all that! I am fascinated this person took time to even notice me and I sometimes wonder why they would want to do that and it is then I realise that person is . . . me! My story highlights the need for self acceptance, self awareness, self encouragement, and self appreciation. It's not advocating narcissism or consumer arrogance, but a healthy recognition of one's talents and abilities.

You see, there are too many women who feel they do not match up to the impossible demands of an image-based society when, if they would just take time, they would see they not only pass the benchmark, they have the ability—and the right—to set their own standards and walk their journey with no apologies—just self acceptance!

In taking time to stop and review my journey thus far, I've had to sit still in amazement and say "Hey, just look at me now!" You see, I may not have "made it" by the world"s standards, but when you were not expected to even leave first base, making it to where I now stand is truly an amazing feat! Who would ever have believed I'd end up here, at this place and time, looking like I do! Wow! In looking back over my life thus far, the nuances and up and downs of an ordinary woman with some extraordinary happenings, **is** truly amazing. If this were someone else's life story, I'd probably throw up my hands, roll my eyes and think "yeah, right!" Truth be told, it's only because life has granted me a chance to sit down, to rest and be still in order for me to take the time sort through the baggage collection I've acquired thus far on this, my journey, that I have been able to come full term and give birth.

Journey Pause: *However, unlike a regular birth where with one push and it's all over (or so I've been told!), in the sharing of my journey thus far, please remember I am a work in progress. I am still moving from my here and now into new and uncharted waters. Birthing this* *little baby is just one aspect of the journey to date. I know there is still a lot more pushing, groaning, straining, sweating (and even swearing!) to do, in order to bring out what else is left within. This is also true for you. As you read this journey, may the birthing of who and what you are intensify and gather pace . . .*

Present Phase:

Mine is the story of a forty-something lady (and yes, I deserve that moniker!), who is twenty-something at heart. Often describing myself as being on the 'mature side' of 25, I am in an interesting position where I live at home (or should it be that my Mum is living with me?), although how I describe my status often depends on my mood, the "moment" and whether or not I want to impress someone! Suffice to say that, for now, we "live together".

Journey Pause: *It's a strange concept in today's modern society because according to current mores, I should be married, living with someone, have children (or at least getting in some serious practice!) but nope; that's my current status right there! I must confess and be honest with you—home life is just too nice! Imagine excellent home-cooked meals on tap, breakfast in bed (and I don't even have to be sick!), someone who'll always love me, a listening ear and I don't even have to "answer" to anyone but moi! What more could a girl want . . . !?! Read on and you'll find out . . . !*

However, do not let my brevity fool you: on my life's journey there have been many instances when I've tried to escape my surroundings in order to forge my own path in life, to create my own destiny. To flee the proverbial nest for a chance to exhibit my own home-making skills without Momma's help; to essentially try to find and "be" me. There have been instances along my journey when I have brought someone into my current home circumstances as a means of escaping—or at least pretending—I was living a "normal" life by trying to be in a "normal" relationship.

You see, I just did not want to be me; I was living and wanting to live my life according to societal benchmarks, in order to "fit in". Yes, there have been many, many times where I wanted to escape the loneliness and heartache I was experiencing. Don't get me wrong, I *was* happy, but only God alone knew the deep-seated longing I had to share an intimacy I'd only ever dreamt and glimpsed in the show window of other people's lives. (More about that later, because I share my thoughts and experiences, I believe someone—maybe you—will hopefully begin to realise they are not alone on their own personal life journey, but will be encouraged that someone else faced similar situations and circumstances—and managed to make it through . . .)

Career wise, I currently work for a trade union; power to the people and all that! It may not be much but it is sufficient to keep the wolves at bay. Given the current economic landscape, with government job cuts and a fall in membership, believe me when I say I am very grateful for it! For several reasons, I have not included the lessons gained during my work career (which is definitely material for another book, trust me!). However, I must say my travels thus far in this area have seen me, a woman of colour (and with glasses!), go through the minefield of employment, displacement and expected under-achievement to finally achieving a sense of finding myself. However, I was to discover my traversing led me to a different destination from that which I had originally programmed into my personal GPS system!

My 'piece de resistance' is my active involvement in the women's ministry group at my local church. This is where my journey has taken me to and is not where I actually started from. I am positively passionate about women, which is a statement you don't hear often from another woman! What and who we are, and what and who we can become, excites me and I want to pass on my enthusiasm to all women that I meet! As President for the women's group, I have to admit I get a buzz and an outer body experience when I say it. Why? Not because of the accolades, acclamations and applause I might receive, but because, knowing where I have been, who I was and seeing how God has ordered my steps thus far, to get to this level, is a miracle and a mystery all at once!

Journey Pause: *Before I continue, I just want to say that I am completely sold out, head-over-heels, madly, badly and gladly in love. Who is the* *object of my affections? Who is the beau who's got me singing love songs late at nights? Who has put a spring in my step and a sparkle in my eye? Who is the One who has stolen my heart? (Well, what I am about to say may come across as religious fanaticism, legalism and just plain old religious rubbish to some, but hey, this is my journey experience!) I know it is not the "done" thing to admit and to voice the following nowadays, but hey, here goes . . . !*

"I am simply sold out for God, completely bowled over by Jesus and wrapped and tied up by the Holy Spirit!"

Phew, well now I have gotten that off my chest, please excuse and allow me a little indulgence at this point. If you are not used to such open expressions, just look on it as a contraction pain and a timely birth pang. However, I do hope the sharing of such intimate knowledge will help you to understand the 'where and whys' of my journey thus far . . . .

Don't get me wrong, it was not always like that. You see, in spite of a love for God, good church teaching and a loving, caring mother, there came a point when I wanted, no I *needed*, to experience things I'd previously been taught against. (I was of those children who had to *feel* the painful results of situations in order to know, by bitter experience what I being warned from and against!) My religious upbringing was not enough to keep me from wanting to find and experience love, acceptance, understanding and confidence—albeit in all the wrong places. Believe me, it really takes courage to allow others into the "birthing room" with you, because as you go through the process, you are most vulnerable, exposed and helpless, for who knows what others may say and see about you?

So, you may ask, why exactly am I doing this; what *is* my modus operandi? It's because, in the religious arena, a lot of women like me, are very good at "fronting". We have a professional, spiritual façade, where we look the part but don't have the courage to step up to the mic and admit to ourselves, much less to others that "Yes, I've been there, I've done that". Although the steps of my journey may not be one you will ever walk, we all recognise life is a road we are all walking, and there some experiences which are common to all. In acknowledging and pointing out the various pitfalls I have fallen into (time and time again), could well be a faint alarm, a final signal to alert fellow travellers, from falling into the same traps.

I am therefore passionate about reminding other women especially those of faith, to know they are not alone in their journey towards their God-ordained destiny. I want to encourage them they are not ordinary or average but special. To encourage them to see themselves as a crystal glass and not a plastic cup, to be used and then thrown away!

So to reiterate, as an "ordinary" woman, my story is not one of drug abuse, prostitution, abortion, but the pain and reality of the old adage of "looking for love in all the wrong places". It is about trying to find myself when I really didn't know what or who I was looking for. It is about opening a door, *that* door, the *secret* door to my inner Self, hoping that the glimmer of light coming through may help a sista behind me. It is about looking for my father in the arms of so many pretenders as I often misinterpreted a look, a whisper . . . a touch . . . in order to be "Daddy's Girl". I know I am not alone in this, but I recognise my journey is about realising that who and what I was ultimately seeking and looking for, was always with me and within me.

Birthing this is about touching the heart of women who have bled themselves to death while wearing a smile and doing "God's work". These women throw themselves into church, social and civil work, seeking to "give back" without ever being replenished themselves. It's for the "singles" (aka unmarried ones) as well as those who are married, but who behind closed doors and with a silent, unresponsive spouse, can and do still feel single and alone. It is for the professional woman, the "supa-woman" trying to multi-task and juggle all that life is throwing at her but who is inwardly terrified she is going to, somehow, someday, come crashing down . . . . It is also for the divorced, the separated and the elderly and also those who feel displaced, like the proverbial square peg in a round hole. It is for all of the above and for those who are inwardly, secretly, wanting to know who God really is and if He even exists . . . It is for all who yearn to know if they can ever really belong and fit in, somewhere, anywhere.

It is about women who have only ever wanted someone, *anyone*, to love them for themselves and because they do not know who they are, they have never known or recognised that they are already loved. It is for every woman who has woken up next to some "man" only to realise the nightmare is real, because heated midnight promises always fade in the cold chill of the morning.

So, to all women, young and old, rich and poor, black and white, I extend an invitation to walk a portion of this journey with me, in the hope you will allow the healing touch of God, the One Who walks and has always walked with you, to minister to you. May you begin to see and realise your journey to where you currently are, has not been in vain.

So, it's back to the beginning, for every journey has a beginning and I invite you to join me at this junction, for where I have been, you might have yet to walk . . . .

So come, take a little walk with "She Who Walks Alone . . . with One".

SECOND INTRODUCTION

"STARTING AGAIN!"

Starting Again.

It's interesting how life will happen until you get it right! I had been "writing" my book for over 5 years now (albeit in my mind), before I finally decided to put pen to paper, or in this case, finger to keyboard. My initial efforts were tentative at first but it was in 2010 when I started to write in earnest. As previously stated, it was my sister DD and then my work colleague, M, who propelled me forward. I started to write and you know when something feels just "right"? Well, that was how it felt for me. It was truly a cathartic process, for each time I would open up and pour out my experiences, thoughts and perspectives, the healing would come and continue, even after the pen was laid to rest.

I began in earnest and was on course but after the first "draft", I became complacent at best and downright lazy at worst! Like raindrops rolling down a window pane, so excuse followed excuse. I would promise myself to write after I'd just watch this "one programme", only to find that four or five hours later, I was ready to fall into bed. Okay, I will write first thing in the morning; but when your circadian rhythm is that of an "owl", trying to get *first thing in the morning* to write is practically going against nature. Thus it was, in the process of recording my life journey I slowed down, stumbled and eventually got lost!

Journey Pause*: Isn't that always the way; armed with the right tools, a map, a compass and the latest GPS system, it is still possible to become so self-confident and self-assured, that you can lose your way—which is what happened to me. I "lost" my initial sense of vision, the drive and passion* *which had initially propelled me in the first place. I "lost" my sense of purpose, as I allowed time to run away with me, instead of structuring and using it to accomplish what I believe I had to do. I almost "lost" my self-integrity, because in making and breaking promises to myself, I was inevitably lying to myself and training myself for future failure.*

However, life has a way of sending its own reminders and post-it notes to ensure you get back on track . . . and so life decided to help me along. In the midst of all my posturing and excuses, in the midst of my oh-so-busy-deadlines, timelines (but seldom lifelines), I lost my USB memory stick. What a lesson right there—this was a major road block! It was comparable to a mudslide on a summer's day—completely unexpected, overwhelming and life changing. Melodramatic maybe, but it was all that and more for me! You see, I had become complacent with the opportunity life had given me to share my journey. I felt, like we all do at times, that time (and the USB!) would always be there. I was always "working" towards an ever-shifting deadline which, for those of you on your own journey, must recognize is a dangerous thing, especially if *you're* the one changing the goalposts.

The USB memory stick, something the size of my little finger, was the repository of my life, to date. I mean it had e.v.e.r.y.t.h.i.n.g—apart from my shoe and dress size—stored on it. To say I was devastated would be a classic example of understatement. However, these things always reveal who we are to ourselves—**if** we're willing to learn the lesson. (Didn't I tell you life has a way of getting our attention!) I found I couldn't pray or even verbalise how I felt (don't laugh; it was more than a memory stick, believe me!) When I realized I had really lost it, I sent an SOS to "The Sistas".

Now, "The Sistas" are those women in my life, who help monitor and operate my emotional 999 helpline. I call them when things are good and in this case, when things are bad, real bad. I sent a text asking them to pray about my loss and yes, I have to admit I was hoping the missing article would turn up, wrapped in angel dust, on the end of my bed but hey, I can dream, can't I! A week later, when it was still on the missing person list, I decided to ask for prayer at my local church. Listen, I figured that if God can make a donkey talk, then He's just gotta be interested in my missing "USB stick", and once again at this point, life stepped in to reassure me. As I stood there, sobbing my heart out and not really caring what people thought (because let's face it, who could ever imagine being so emotionally distraught over a mere IT item?), the minister said that, if God knew where Saul's donkeys were, He surely knew where this item was. Now, this may not mean anything to you but what was said really helped to reassure me. I began to realize that a missing USB stick "don't stop no show" for the source of this book had come from within me and was therefore still available and accessible; all I had to do was start again.

Journey Pause: *Reader: stop and re-read that point again! You've tried and tried again but it just won't work. Maybe all you need to do it to review it from another angle, a fresh perspective and simply . . . start all over again . . .*

Well, that is what I did and added it as my second "introduction". No, it was not easy trying remember and to replicate structures, sentences and sentiments. Nope, it was not easy trying to find time to make up time to meet my personal deadline, nor having to relive situations and events on a deeper and intimate level. But I did it—and so can you! As you read this, please keep in mind that, no matter how bad it looks no matter how bad it gets, no matter how bad it IS, you can . . . you MUST . . . you have no choice but to "start again". Trust me: it may never be the same but it can (and will) be better the second time around . . . .

Welcome once again to "She Who Walks Alone . . . with One!"

CHAPTER 2

Precious Memories

"Precious memories how they linger! How they ever
flood my soul.

In the stillness of the midnight, precious memories
still unfold . . ."

In walking my life journey, there are many times when I've sat down to review and reflect on past memories. What always makes me smile is knowing those memories, which at the time were the cause of so much heartache, pain and angst, are "precious memories" I can now sing about! So in this brief chapter, I'd like to share a few of those memories with you. They may not seem like much and indeed, may seem humdrum and rather mediocre, but trust me, they are the reason why I am here, and maybe, just maybe, they will be able to help you look back and recognise your own "precious memories".

Way back, I mean way, way back, when pounds, shillings and pence was the national currency and neighbours said hello to each other and summers were hot and winters were cold, when I look back, the one thing that stands out for me is—my Mum. Not a surprising fact as I am her only child, but it's the memories of the special love she had (and still has) for me, which I remember as a child being demonstrated in pillow fights, which Mum always started and which would end in hugs, tickles, and lots and lots of love and laughter. Yes, that's a very "precious memory" for me.

Another "precious memory" is the first foster carer I stayed with, Mrs. L. As a pre-toddler, Mrs L. taught me the alphabet and it was there my precociousness and sense of wanting to colour out the box emerged. "'A" for apple, "B" for bat, "C" for cat'" was how I would always start but when I got to "K" for kettle, I'd always say "cup of tea, cup of tea"—how cute is that—not! Nowadays I'd probably be sent to remedial school for not knowing the correct answer for the letter "K", when all I was doing was developing my unique send of wanting to interpret things my way. Maybe it was sign of my trying to express my individuality, who knows, but it's a memory which, for some reason, flashes as a definite journey marker in my mind.

Another precious and still enduring memory relates to food, where I was my Mum's official taster. This factor has I believe, has laid a sure foundation for my roller-coaster love affair with all things edible (well, most things, not all!) Not for me the quintessential delights of English cuisine featuring high-tea and "meat and two veg", oh no! Mine was of the exotic, tangy and spicy variety with real Trinidadian classics such as "Mauby", a bitter-sweet drink which I did not like then but can't get enough of now. Mum would always put some "essence" in it; either aniseed or pear and it always had to be served shaken not stirred (honestly!) with lots of ice. "Sorrel", a berry-red tangy drink was another traditional Trinidadian favourite, which Mum would sometimes spice up with fresh ginger. I remember bottles and bottles of it being prepared at Christmas, because the season was not complete without it.

Ah Christmas, now *that* was a serious occasion for our large household of two! In our tiny flat, Mum would bring the taste, flavours and atmosphere of her Caribbean home (Trinidad & Tobago) right to Essex, with a vast variety of roasts, rice dishes (yes, plural!), steaming bowls of vegetables and the above drinks. Added to the now groaning table would be a bottle or two of "Chateau de Mum", some of Mum's home brew.

Now Mum had a knack of making a "little something" from practically anything! She was au fait with making the usual homemade grape wines . . . but could she stop there? As if! I remember being sent to a special corner to the larder to retrieve bottles of mysterious looking liquids, which were all stacked together in a dark corner, congregating as if they were having a clandestine illegal meeting. One was named "Plum"; another "Apricot"; another "Raspberry" and so on. Mum's wine making paraphernalia was DIY to say the least but boy, were the results good (hic!)

Like a lot of little girls at the time, I remember having very own little mixing bowl with its very own small wooden spoon for my own use whenever Mum was making a cake and yes, I even had my very own cake tin; small, short, round and cute, just like the owner! From the rickety oven, Mum would produce yet more Caribbean delicacies: coconut tarts made from melt-in-the-mouth pastry stuffed full with freshly grated coconut (None of that dried stuff for my Mum; oh no, it had to be the real McCoy, the proper, I-have-to-break-and-crack-you-open-and-grate-you-down fresh coconut), spices, vanilla and/or almond essence and a clove or two for added flavour.

Sometimes, Mum would add a drop or two of red colouring and I'd be surprised and delighted by either white or pink coconut tarts. Trust me, when it comes to food, I was taught not to discriminate on colour—just taste...! Coconut drops and other coconut-related homemade goodies are enduring memories (I think my Mum really had a thing for coconut!).

And then, there's my all time favourite: roti, which is a mildly seasoned, thinly rolled bread NOT to be confused with chapatti, never! No, the Trini version is a thinner, chapatti-like version, which often has a spicy split-pea filling. Listen, the smell of chicken, goat or any type of curry with a sheet or two (or more, let me honest here!) of the aforementioned roti, was enough to send me into orbit—or at least for another helping! Now *that's* what I call authentic "finger lickin'" good food!"

Macaroni pie was another one. Now, for those who are not au fait with Caribbean culture, 'macaroni pie' is more commonly known as 'macaroni cheese'. My description of simple "mac and cheese" was a source of deep debate and intrigue when I was at school, as I was often teased for calling 'macaroni cheese' by its Caribbean vernacular, 'macaroni pie', where my fellow English school friends thought it was pasta and cheese in encased in short crust pastry. Please!

The first time I had it was during a 'Home Economics' lesson (now that is a real ol' fashioned term right there, nowadays it's probably Urban

Cooking 101!), I couldn't understand why we needed to add flour to the milk to make a "roux sauce" before adding the cheese and pasta nor why was no additional seasoning other than salt and pepper was ever allowed . . . arrgh! For me, the *proper* way was, once the pasta had been cooked, to fry some onions (and peppers if feeling particularly adventurous!), add a little milk and a LOT of cheese. Reader, I'm talking blocks of cheese, of the cholesterol-soaring, artery-busting variety! Yes, huge amounts of the stuff would be added to milk and voila, that was authentic cheese sauce! Add the pasta, stir and pop in the oven with yes, you've guessed it, more cheese on the top. Ohh, and let's not forget the "seasoning" which had to be incorporated.

Journey Pause: As a "Tringlish" girl (English born-Trinidadian culture!), "seasoning" was—and still is—an integral part of my life. Everything, from the humble baked bean to a full-on traditional roast has to have "seasoning". As Mum always made her own seasoning, you know which one had to go into the dish. When I began to cook, comments like "hmm, it ain't tasting too bad but you know, I think something missing . . . you put in any seasoning?" would make me sigh, roll my eyes and go for the jar with Mama's homemade seasoning and, truth to be told, the dish would always taste better—but don't tell her I said so! On reflection, I think her seasoning made every dish so special and tasty because love was the key ingredient in all her cooking. How many of us have tried to replicate our own Mum's cooking and just can't seem to get it tasting the same way, even when we've followed the recipe, ounce for ounce and herb for herb? Seriously, I believe mothers are programmed to put love and care into each dish and that's why I want to be able to cook like my Mama!)

So now, as I flick through the pages of yesteryear and relive past milestones on my journey to the here and now, I have to stop and smile as I unfold the memory of my first ever "boyfriend".

First Boyfriend . . . Ahhh!

At that time, safe within the confines of a loving and perhaps, an over-protective church and home environment, I was not one of the popular girls. Now don't get me wrong; I had many friends; you know those ol' faithful childhood friends who knew you 'back in the day'; those who started out with you and with whom you can just 'be' yourself. These are friends who, even after several years, you can simply pick up and catch up where you left off however long ago. Yep, I'm sure you know the type I mean!

As church was a major and integral part of my social life there were several large families who attended in those days and we'd all just hang out as one big happy family. Okay, it wasn't quite the "Waltons" or "Little House on the Prairie", but you get my drift. Now, regarding boyfriends, dating and ooohhh, relationships", (tremble, tremble!), in those days, I was content to look but never venture past that point (not that I ever got or even had a chance!)

Yet I remember my first "crush" (*or "squeeze" as I liked to term them, as, according to my terminology, a "squeeze" was not a serious as a "crush", with a "squeezette", being somewhere between the two. Told you I liked to colour outside the box, ha ha ha!*)

Now I liked someone in the "group". He was a couple of years older than me, a real live teen-ager, with lips that could suck the bark off a tree (oh yes!). He had a lean and lanky I need-to-eat physique and NHS tortoiseshell spectacles which intensified his (already) big eyes and lovely lashes, to me, he was just so, well, handsome and intelligent. Oh, I made sure kept my "lurve" for him well hidden because believe me, the other kids could be cruel if they even just got a 'whiff' of weakness; talk about a pack mentality—however, I digress.

Journey Pause: *Ahhh, the first memory of your first squeeze, your first crush and your first love. You were able to look past the pimples, flairs, the NHS glasses and all that other stuff, to the hunk that wore them. Dental braces only just enhanced his smile; facial acne was merely a game of "join-the-dots" waiting to be played; a skinny frame enhanced his intelligence (huh!) whilst an over-large frame just gave you a little something more to hug. Remember when just hearing his voice would send you into orbit; when a stray glimpse from him in your direction would cause you to write pages and pages in your 'secret diary' (and don't bother to don't deny you had one!). Remember when you would* *strategically position yourself just to be near him and it was all you needed? When you didn't need him to touch or talk to you because, just being in the same room and breathing the same air, was enough? Oh, stop looking at me as if you don't remember; okay then, maybe it was just me! Anyway, ahem, let me continue my "Precious Memories"!*

It was a Saturday evening at my friend's house, where it was the norm for us to have post-service gatherings, where our families would come together for fun and fellowship. Whilst the adults were catching up the latest happenings in "Dallas" or "Dynasty", we were in another room, dealing with the more serious issues relevant to people of our own age.

After sometime, I became aware of a lot of whispering, talking and giggling amongst the others and when you're not involved, it's a safe assumption you're the one on the menu and yes, I was all too right, gulp! I was asked to leave the room (don't think I had a choice!) and I heard bursts of laughter as soon as the door closed. When I was finally summoned to come back in, I was asked if I noticed anything or *anyone* was missing.

Being nervous and not wanting to be the centred of attention, I was unsure if this was a trick question or not and tried hard to look nonchalant but I think my shaky knees and slight stammering gave me away. I then noticed P___ wasn't anywhere to be seen and there was no way he could have passed me, as I had been on sentry duty outside. The penny dropped and so I managed to ask where he was. He rose from behind the settee, blushing furiously (whoever said Black people don't blush aren't looking properly—or just don't' know where to look!). By this time, everyone was laughing and I felt ready to die on the spot because I knew that somehow and in some way I'm involved and P is involved and wait, was that *romance* I was smelling?.

P___ was probably feeling worse than myself and he looked like he was ready to pass out behind his NHS glasses, but bless him, he managed to pluck up the courage to ask me to go outside—into the hallway, I might add—as he had something to say. With a beating heart I followed, thinking . . . if this was . . . could this be it? Was he going to ask the question I'd dreamed and written about for ages in my secret diary? Was it possible I was finally, at long, long, *long* last, going to get a bonafide boyfriend, someone who liked me and wanted to be seen with me (Sista, remember that last thought; it's very significant . . .).

We stepped into the dimly light hallway. P__ shut the door and amidst much stuttering and stammering, he managed to "ask me out". Now, I'll always treasure the memory because it represents the golden age of innocence. At 14, I was slightly older than his tender 13-years. (On hindsight, I think I was setting a trend for my future but when "lurve" is involved, age ain't nothin' but a number.) Well of course I said "yes" and we went back inside, to whoops, cheers and giggles. That was it; my being "asked out" experience. Now, what we were supposed to *do* no one ever told us, hahaha! Wow! It was all I could have hoped and longed for; a love struck hero (13 year old P___), an unknowing but yearning heroine (me!) and a number of giggling witnesses to verify the truth of it all. You can that was front page headlines in my diary and was my daily review for several "lurve-struck" weeks.

Our "relationship" lasted for a glorious six weeks, during which time we went to the fair and he brought me an ice-cream. Now why that is significant, I don't know; maybe it's because I associate feeling good with food! That was the extent of our "going out": a visit to the fun fair as well as "meeting" up at church, but hey that was all my "lurve" and I needed . . .

Journey pause: *In comparison to then innocence of that age, it seems many of today's youth are nowadays required to be "tooled up" with the right kind of contraceptives and other contraptions before they can be deemed to be in a relationship. Dare parents ever deny them their conjugal human rights, it's an affront to their human rights! Demands for sexual experimentation seems to be starting earlier and earlier, usually at an age where the sexual wanna-be's can't even sell the word, but where society's "do-gooders" are pushing them to know and experience their "sex-u-ali-tee"*

However, back then, holding hands was the most we, (well I), could and would ever dare to do. Mr P___ was a gentleman then and even after we "broke up". I guess like good "relationships", we drifted apart after a wonderful 6 or 7 weeks together of ice-cream, church services and one fairground ride. Yes, I managed to squeeze out the obligatory tear and find a friend's shoulder to cry on. Oh yes, I was now able to join in with school mates about boyfriends and break ups—except I only had the one, whilst they were chalking up their scores on the proverbial head board. Honestly, the break up of "true lurve" at such a young age is very traumatic . . . well, sort of, well, until the next guy comes along, I guess!

(I've since heard that he's now married with a family. Mr P___, I just want to thank you for noticing and treating me as the princess I'd always wanted to be, but never knew I was, at a time when I didn't even know I existed.)

The First Mwah!

Another "precious memory" relates to my first ever . . . kiss. As the saying goes, you never forget your first and was something I felt compelled to add.

Journey Pause: *Sistas, you need to recognise your precious memories have helped to shape and define who and what you are now. Most times we have no control over what happens to us, but one thing I've learned on my journey thus far, is that we can control how we react and what we make of the experience. We control whether to see them as stumbling blocks or stepping stones, obstacles or opportunities for growth. Trust me when I say, the end result is really up to you . . .*

Now walk with me a little further, as I share one of my sweetest "precious memories".

He was a friend, someone I'd practically grown up with. I had liked him since my pre-teens as he was one of the few guys who really noticed me (ahhhh). Ladies, you know how it is; you're a pre-teen with tortoise-shell NHS glasses (no SpecSavers or Vision Express in those days) with the prerequisite pre-teen spots and rather too much puppy fat. I had breasts before I even knew what to do with them (or indeed, what could be done to them . . . but I'll leave that thought right there, thank you).

Yes even within a safe environment like church, like a potato in the dark, my feelings grew and developed for Mr B. He could always (and still does) make me laugh whenever we happen to bump into each other and at there time, these seemed to be a "thing" between us. In growing up, Mr B_____ was always there to listen to my growing pains regarding boys, boys and . . . boys. Which ones I'd like; which one's I thought might like me; which one's I really couldn't stand. Now at the time, having "left church" to discover himself, Mr B would pop back every now and then for a social visit. Over the years, I managed to keep my feelings to myself as, having experienced life, Mr B was now getting what I was not able to give.

Essentially, Mr B_____ was a willing and sympathetic ear, the brother I never had. I enjoyed going to his house to laugh and kick back with him, until one day, it happened. I was at college at the time and had developed yet (another) "this-is-the-real-thing" crush on a guy there. He was of Middle Eastern origin with a little moustache, tall and swarthy looking—basically drop dead gorgeous . . . and he was intelligent. (By the way, I have always been attracted to men who can reason and who have a modicum of some intelligence. Unfortunately my theory has not always held me in good stead, as intelligence doesn't equate to wisdom, honesty and truthfulness)

Having always felt at ease with Mr B and his family (his mother knew Mum and just loved me!), it was not a problem to drop by and hang out in his bedroom, where I'd offset my problems. By this time, Mr B had become very "knowledgeable" about life, sex and all that jazz, so talking to him now became informative. Like a well-paid psychiatrist he'd ask me deep and probing questions like why don't you tell him how you feel, to which I'd invariably blush and stammer a reply that there was no way I could let my latest crush (or squeeze!) know how I felt, as I just didn't think it was the right thing to do. He would then give his usual dazzling smile and ask "but why, Shalis?" and I would then proceed to expound my theory as to how girls are supposed to wait and men are supposed to do the chasing—a la Mills & Boon—and our relationship counselling session would be over—until my next "lurve crisis" arose.

On this memorable occasion, it was the same scenario. I was having my usual appointment at Mr. B's "office", pouring out my heart about my latest crush when he moved from his chair to sit next to me on the bed. Have you ever had a moment when all of the sudden, the air is sucked out of the room and you're left literally struggling to inhale let alone exhale? Well, that is what happened: I was breathless and experiencing what old-fashioned novel writers would term, a "heaving bosom" moment. The room was quiet; sun light was pouring in and he sat next to me . . . and all my childhood feelings for Mr. B___ came rushing back. It's either that Mr. B___ was a smooth operator or I was extremely naïve—or it was a dangerous combination of both . . .

"Shalisa, why don't you tell him how you feel?"

"Are you crazy? You must be joking! Never"

"Shalisa, what if he held your hand?"

"Me? I'd pass out!" (In case you've not picked up on this, I was painfully shy when around members of the opposite sex).

"Well, what if he did this?" . . . . and that's when it happened. Mr. B slowly placed his lips on mine and kissed me, gently, tenderly and deeply.

I remember his—our bodies—trembling and I knew I'd never forget this special, tender and unforgettable moment . . . . . Our doctor-patient relationship was quickly dissolved that day and little did I know I was beginning to forge an indelible, inevitable path on my journey. This was not a long-term relationship but it was, for me, an introduction to the potential sweetness life and love can offer. Sadly, I was yet to learn that what is sweet can often leave a bitter aftertaste . . .

We have kept in touch over the years and when we bump into each other, there's always a little "something" between us, an undeniable magnetism. We both know and have joked about it over the years . . . and I had often wondered (and hoped for) a more lasting and a permanent "precious moment" with my very own, Mr. B, but thankfully, our journey tastes can and do change directions over the years . . . !

Wow, there are still boxfuls of precious memories to sort through: my first car, my first job where I remember blowing my weekly wages at Covent Garden market . . . and the first time I got my hair "relaxed", on my first trip to the Caribbean. Now, let me share a little anecdote with you about *that* . . .

Final Net

I was invited to go to Jamaica with my good friend, LL. Marvellous Mandeville was the favoured UK enclave for returning Jamaicans at the time, was where we stayed. My hair was initially in braids for the holiday as I thought it would be easier to maintain, but the heat made it so unbearable and, after much persuasion from my friend and her family, I decided to have it relaxed. (For those of the non Afro-Caribbean persuasion, "relaxing" is a perm used to straighten our hair and is, I guess the opposite of those perms others would use to make their hair curly and wavy. Honestly, we women are never satisfied!)

Now you have to understand my "virgin" hair was soft, natural and thick, very thick. Having been with me all my life, I didn't understand the dramatic change relaxing my hair would have on me—literally. After having it "creamed" (a Jamaican term used when I went for the procedure), I was shocked to find not only could the comb go through my hair without breaking or snagging, but to me, my new found-locks felt and looked like "wet chicken feathers"! Was *this* how it was supposed to look? My hair seemed to lack the body, thickness and weight I'd been used to but hey, it was now shiny, swishy and glossy and, I must admit, looking good too!

As you can imagine, change of any kind takes some getting used too, and this was no exception. Whereas I would need two or three large elastic bands to even begin to coax my hair into a pony tail, I found I only needed a teeny, weeny little one to hold it in place—wow! To get the latest bouffant style, I could now use plastic roll and clip curlers. (Let me tell you, those things are only good if you have a masochistic streak, as they're rock hard and can leave you with a serious headache whenever you try to sleep in them) So, did they work for me? As if! After a sleepless night of tossing and turning and wanting to pull them out just to get, some oh, sweet relief and a couple hours of sleep, I'd wake up, tired and bleary eyed, take out the iron-hard curlers to admire the hoped-for luscious curls, only for my painfully acquired style to flop down around my ears within minutes. Drastic action was needed!

On the advice of my friend's little sister, I decided to try a holding spray called "Final Net". Let me tell you, it was superglue for hair; once held, there was no letting go or getting away from "the Net". So one Friday before going to bed, I decided to try it. I liberally sprayed each section of my soft and silky hair before carefully rolling it up after which, once done, my blue, green and pink-curled hair was safely secured with the ultimate passion-killer head wear, the ubiquitous "stocking top" (now what *that* is, I just ain't tellin' for now!) Why all this preparation; why all this torture? Well, on Saturday, I was going to church to see Bro G, a Black-Chinese Jamaican (now you understand why the sudden need to get my get my hair "creamed"!) Saturday morning arrived and I still recall my outfit; a long white linen dress with a matching linen overcoat; lovely! I tell you, Bro G would not be able to resist my charms.

Journey Pause: *Sistas, let's confess—this is something we all tend to do. I think it's programmed into our gene pool, so don't feel too bad if you recognise this behaviour in yourself! We cut it, style it, wax it, pluck it, reshape and mould it, inject and even cut, tuck and liposuction it, if we deem it necessary. Yes, I'm talking about the things we've done (and still do!) to get a man's attention! The sad is that we're in danger of looking and measuring ourselves through the eyes of someone else instead of celebrating who, what and where we are. Yes, it is good to want to update and change ourselves; yes, it is commendable to want to lose a few pounds, stones and even boulders in some cases, to improve our overall health and overall appearance; and yes, there's nothing wrong in adding shaping a little, putting in/on/off a little—but dear reader, I urge you to please, please, please make sure you do it for that VERY important person—YOURSELF!*

So after some time of careful and meticulous dressing, I took the curlers out and gave another liberal spray of "Final Net". At last I had it: a perfect coiffure, with each curl in its place (remember, this was the Eighties' and the puffed, curly hair look was fashionable, at least in my books anyway). We arrived at the church in Mandeville and I scanned the pews. Ohhh, Bro G was there, looking soooo fine with his brown skin, Chinese eyes and grey suit. After service, my time came.

Bro G saw me and came over (yes!) and I struck what I thought was a casual pose where I decided to run my fingers through my now silken, relaxed and flowing locks—but I didn't reason with the staying power of Final Net. I nonchalantly ran a finger or two from the front of my bouncy bouffant hair style with the intention of just giving a final flick at the back (sistas, you know how we do it!) but alas; it was not to be. Final Net won as it encased my fingers just past my left ear. Sadly, I remember it, oh so well. I wanted to pull my fingers all the way through, but there was no release! I couldn't go back because the Net was too strong for me and I couldn't go forward without messing up my hair. So, I stood there chatting and laughing with Bro G whilst trying to tug my hand out of my hair. It must have looked like a strange dating mating dance, with one hand in my hair, while trying to maintain eye contact and talk to Bro G, as if nothing strange or untoward was happening. My friend's sister finally noticed my dilemma and came over (she told me later she was wondering why I was "standing so stupid and not talking properly to de man"). I'm not sure if I muttered something about my hair but the sweet joke was when Bro G commented on how nice my hair was looking—even as I stood there with my hand in my hair, unable to move or take it out!

My friend's sister had to come to my rescue and literally pulled me out of my hairy predicament and boy, did she and LL laugh when I told them what happened. It was only then she decided to tell me "Shalisa, you only needed a likkle spray, not de whole bokkle!"

It all ended rather well actually as Bro G and I became pen pals and corresponded for sometime; but in spite of "Final Net", I obviously could not "hold" him (groan, groan!)

Well, dear reader, thanks for allowing me to share a few of my precious memories from my life journey. Here's hoping they have helped *you* to remember and reminisce about your own precious memories . . . !

CHAPTER 3

Sandwich Generation: Open-top Filling

Following the previous chapter, this is a good place to bring in this issue.

My mum had me when she was 40 years old. So when I began to surface and desired to start living, Mum was over 60- and that's when the fun started. We were always seen as a mother and daughter package, Bim-and-Bam. When you see one you invariably see the other. There was and still is something in me which struggles to be . . . me; or at least seek an opportunity to do so.

Now this part of my journey relates to those sisters who feel they have given (or have even lost) their substance, their essence, in caring for an elderly parent, a disabled parent, a spouse or child. Whilst it is definitely a labour of love, we have to admit there are times when the "labour" is a more prominent factor. Yet I pray you too will be thankful for the strength which underpins our efforts to be able to love unconditionally, compassionately and faithfully. This is an emotional minefield and not one which many like to admit to themselves, much less to anyone else. When most people (in this case, women) reach a "certain age", they are caught between having to care for their children and their aging parents, hence the term "sandwich generation". I understand the difficulties and emotions that abound, especially for single-parents trying to do it on their own. But if you just take time to listen, you will hear the heart-sigh of the sista-singletons, those unmarried, childless women who quietly and stoically bear the pain of being an "open-topped sandwich". For they give with no thought, knowledge and maybe no expectation of who, if anyone, will be able to reciprocate and/or return the deed, when its their turn to be "laboured" over.

Theirs—"ours"—is a twilight existence. You see, they may have the house, the car, the job and all the other trappings deemed necessary and successful by society and their contemporaries, but deep down inside, there is the pain of having to do it all on their own, without a legacy or heritage to pass it onto. Let me make it personal: ours is the emotional and sometimes painful reality of having to now care for someone who cared for us; of living and experiencing the vagary of life as roles are reversed and the mother or father is the child, the child is the parent and the roller coaster of life now takes a new twist.

As I sit and reminisce at this journey junction, believe me when I say, I understand, I really do. There have been times when I wanted someone, *anyone*, to simply take me away from all of this. When the mundaneness of it all grew too much for me, leaving only the humdrum and mediocrity of the here and now, as the best that one could to look forward to. There were times when I wondered if having a child might even help to shift the focus, to give me a sense of hope and a future, as opposed to seemingly always having to deal with the past. You see, for as long as I can remember, I was told, "You have to look after your mother" "I hope you don't put her in a home", "Remember all the things she did for you". Yes, all these all well-meaning and well-intentioned sentiments only served to increase the pressure and deep-seated angst that was simmering below and deep within.

For me, putting Mum in a home was not even on the radar. From a very young age, I was acutely aware of the sacrifice my Mum had made—and it increased as I grew older. For when love and youth are running through your veins, and life's promises and expectations like gilts and bonds guarantee to yield a rich reward on a given date; when life's summer breeze promises to blow away cobwebs forever, I began to understand, just a little bit, of just how much Mum had given up for me. For to have known love in its secret intimate moments; to have exchanged looks and sighs that only a lover can interpret; to have opened up and looked into another's soul—and then to make a conscientious and determined decision to leave it all behind . . . Hmmm, could I have done the same? *Would* I have done the same? I reasoned and purposed that I should; I could; I *would* have to do so, as Mum had no one else to look after her. I knew it was my expected role and responsibility, but within, deep inside, well meaning intentions daily fought against natural urges and desires.

Apparently, I must have had some foresight about this turn of events, for when I was younger, I used to tell Mum that I would feed her, give her chocolate and wash and "powder her bam-bam" when she grew older.

Journey Pause: *Strange how children can pick up and 'tune in' to future events, circumstances and situations. What clarity we all had in our innocent years, when everything was crystal clear to our young minds. Sad that life, societal norms and other soul-breaking experiences work to break that out of us. What do we need to do to re-find and regain that sense of assurance, calmness and propriety once again? Did you foresee you would be where you are now or did you have another, a much bigger dream? This is just a timely "journey pause" to let you know you can still recreate a dream, **your** dream and start today . . . .*

At the age of 29, we moved. At the time, I was working full time and studying part-time for my degree, which was akin to working two full-time job, let me tell you! Like most young women, I dreamed of love, marriage and "happily ever after" (aka Mills & Boon again!) and was even collecting for my "bottom drawer". One day, as I adding yet another silver-plated hors d'oeuvre dish to my horde, I had an "ahha moment"! I was not in a "serious" relationship with anyone at the time and it's then the rose-coloured glasses just fell off. Prince Charming was *not* about to whisk me away from my council flat door, clasp me to his manly bosom and kiss me as we rode off into the sunset on his white steed (aka BMW or Mercedes Benz!).

I therefore decided to start using the few "bottom drawer" items I'd collected thus far and to make a concerted effort to change my—our—lives. As mentioned before, Mum had recently retired around this time and financially, life was not easy but I guess I just never knew it or knew the extent of it! Although I never had the latest this or that, I had lots and lots of love. Yet, growing up and seeking to develop and bloom into your own self is a major force which propels you into wanting to make changes, hopefully for the better.

The personal vision and driving force which propelled me, was to one day see Mum come home from a hard day's shopping, drop into a chair and simply "cock up" (i.e. to put up and to rest!) her foot. This dream stayed with me for years and years and was watered with many tears and prayers. I also realised with time and age, things would not always be the same, especially regarding Mum's health and the fact that where we lived had no lift facilities. Yes, with Mum being a recent retiree and me working, it was truly late spring and late autumn in the house, as we were two women walking out our own respective journeys in different seasons.

When we moved (see Chapter 6 for the painful experience), I busied myself with the task in hand. I have to thank God for His mercy, grace and goodness, because when I look back, only God could have brought and kept us thus far. A few years after the move, Mum had a fall in a local convenience store which worsened any health and mobility problems she might have had—but was not confessing to!

Journey Pause: *We are all shaped by the examples before us. My Mum was a quintessential "SBW"—strong, Black woman! She could come in from night work (she was a midwife), paint and redecorate a room, move furniture, change the furnishings, wash, iron, cook a gourmet dinner, go shopping (Mum's love for all things market is legendary!), grab a "power nap" before having to get ready to go to work the next night! She just did not rest; I mean, when she wasn't doing that, she was busy cooking something for someone, somewhere. But don't you know the body has a way of letting you know when it's time to just STOP and be still? Mum's health problems were, I strongly believe, related to her reticence to rest; take a break and, most importantly, to put herself FIRST, every now and then. Dear Sista, just pause here to consider where you are and how you are treating that most important person in your life—YOU! When was your last check up? When was your last holiday? When was the last time you turned off the phone, lit a candle or two, poured yourself a nice, ice-cold drink, played some soothing soul music and was still . . . soul still? Your running around now may well have painful consequences later on; don't wait for life send a painful reminder—you have been warned . . . !*

Despite my many protestations for her to go to the doctor, she really endeavoured to carry on as usual; perhaps she felt going to the doctor would be admitting a weakness or failure, I don't know. After Mum had retired, she still worked part-time and having taken up art classes, was really developing into a budding artist. However after the fall, it wasn't just her mobility which seemed to slow down and stop, but in some way her desire to create, to go on and dare I say, to live, seemed to dwindle as well.

Journey Pause: *Yes, you knew I was stopping here! What was it that made you stop and in some cases turn back? You got married, had children, studied, got a job—even lost a pound or two—but, hmmm, something is still missing. What was it that has hindered and is still hindering you from developing, growing and becoming who you dreamed of being? If you have fully attained ALL that you had dreamed, my sista, I applaud you! But if, like so many of us, you've had a "fall"—whatever and where it may have been—I encourage you to get back up again and get back on your journey. I especially encourage you to discover (or re-discover) your creative side. Write a poem. Draw (even if it's matchstick men and women, hey you did it; be proud). Sing. To yourself. (Don't laugh, it's all about sparking and kick-starting your creative bent! Although you may want to do it softly and by yourself at first, okay!). Join a knitting, sewing, cake baking and/or decorating class—whatever takes your fancy, but DO something (even write a book!). Why? Because it helps in the development of the whole person, it's a great de-stressor and who knows, you might even be able to make something out of it. And when you retire and no longer have to take two trains, one tube and four buses to work, you can continue doing what you're doing now—which is loving and developing your creative self . . . and doesn't that sound wonderful! Opps sorry, I've kept you long enough; let's get back to remembering my journey past . . .*

I remember the painful episode when I took Mum to our then-family doctor, Doctor D . . . . . . After months and months of persuasion, she finally agreed to see him. She could hardly walk as we shuffled into his surgery. Mum explained the situation and requested physiotherapy. Doctor D's response and diagnosis was for Mum to "get some trainers and go for a walk!" He obviously ignored the fact she simply could not walk unaided, as I was her walking 'aid' for some time, and also overlooked the glaring fact that she was walking in a lot of pain. I sat there in his clinical, cold office, choking back tears of anger and hurt. I was just so angry this man, a *doctor*, could be so casually dismissive and I was also hurt, for I felt impotent to say and do anything. Nor did I want to talk in case tears came instead of words . . . and even remembering the pain of that moment, that time, is still tangible. I felt alone and helpless for I had no one to help, no one to stand with me and no one to argue our case. Such loneliness and helplessness is further worsened when you are caring and carrying someone else. Sista, I just want to reassure you at as this point, whether you're in a loveless marriage, whether you're a single parent, whether you have care responsibilities for an elderly parent—whatever your particular and personal situation, please remember—you are not alone.

Mum and I shuffled out of the surgery, each nursing our own and each other's disappointment, with me leaning on her as much as she was leaning on me. I don't think we ever saw "Dirty Doctor D . . . ." again, as I then called him, for not long afterwards, Mum told me he died.

When I've discussed that time with Mum, she believes she might have had a slight stroke, because her left foot would drag as if she had no control over it. For it me, I saw it as a sign of what was to come—a sense of inevitability. I felt trapped; for at a time when I felt I should have been moving forward, growing, flourishing and even considering marriage, I was thinking about and looking into wheelchairs, walking sticks, physiotherapy and Zimmer frames—just what every young woman has in mind . . . Not! (Now who I would or could have married, I really don't know, because I never seemed to date anyone who was serious enough about me—or vice versa!).

One memorable occasion was when Mum, who was becoming severely disabled, now begun to acknowledge her mobility problems. From someone who loved to shop and who was a regular market goer, Mum was becoming more and more confined to the house—and to bed. Mum, who could cook up a storm in a blink of an eye, would limp from kitchen sink to cooker and back again, taking painful minutes to do what used to be done in a matter of moments. Arthritis became more noticeable in her hands and old pains began to flare up once again and I mainly confided my concerns with DD. Yes, it is good to talk but you have to know *who, when* and *where* to talk to. For while you may be looking for sympathy and even empathy it helps to speak to the right people who can actually *help* your situation. Thankfully, I was blessed to have such a person in DD. She advised me on the relevant benefits Mum was entitled to. I must add at this point that, prior to this episode, Mum had NEVER applied for any social security, not even child benefit for me. When I had once asked why, she explained that at the time, you were expected to "open your soul and sell your guts" just to get a few pence—and she did not think it was worth it; good ol' Trini pride!

Thanks to the advice given, I was able to apply for and thankfully receive the necessary application forms for Mum to fill in. Little did I know what would follow, for it is then I came face-to-face with the legendary Anthony stubbornness: Mum simply refused to look at them, much less sign them! This was to become a the regular pattern: I would take them to her and explain that, given her physical situation, she was entitled to x, y and z and all she had to do was to sign here, here and there; but when I returned came to collect what I thought were completed forms, I would find them on the bed or the table in pristine condition and still in the envelopes, practically untouched, just as I had given them to her. Wow! Talk about frustration! Then coupled with this fiasco, I had deal with well-meaning people asking me "So, what's happening with Mum? What are you doing about it? You should get your Mum to apply for help, you know? What are you doing about it?" What was *I* doing about it?!!?!! At those times, I would have to literally grin and bear it. Can you imagine the pain of being made to feel so inadequate and incompetent when behind closed doors, all my ranting and raving, pleading and pouting couldn't get Mum to pick up a pen, much less to sign the form!?!

I would then cry, shout and talk to DD loudly (all designed for Mum to hear, of course,) and so repeat the cycle. The feeling of being trapped in a situation not of my own making would increase, as I felt this scenario was my lot in life: knocking at Mum's door only to be ignored and rejected. As I review this journey juncture, I think Mum was probably depressed about the whole situation and my constant badgering could not have helped, but don't get me wrong; I tried various approaches from choleric to phlegmatic to see if she would co-operate. Mum's (now) famous line "alright, alright, in a minute dear, I'll do it in a minute" began to wear very, very thin. Remember, she was retired and I was now working in the public sector and the little money (literally) had to cover mortgage, insurance and all the essentials necessities that accompany being a "home owner", including the "poll tax"! To top it all, I started to indulge an inherent need to look good as a reaction to what was going on around and within me. I didn't want to be seen and deemed as frumpy and dowdy before my time, whenever and whatever that was! Within myself, I felt being an unofficial carer meant my "essence" was being sucked away and I did not want to get old too soon without experiencing the sweetness of youth and all it had to offer.

But thank God, help was at hand, in the form of one of Mum's friend, Mrs C____. She asked about Mum and what I was doing about her situation. Me? ME! Previously, I would have said "Mum's taking it easy", and "God is with us"; you know, the usual bland comments, because let's face it; I really did not want to bring to the surface the pain, hurt and sense of inadequacy I was feeling because I felt I had failed and was failing in my duties as a "good daughter". Surely a good and caring daughter would have sorted things out a lot sooner because it got the stage where began to ask myself "hey Shalisa, what exactly ARE you doing about the situation!?!" But this time, I decided to come clean, open up and just tell Mrs. C____ the truth of where I was; how, in spite and despite my attempts to talk to Mum, despite the numerous forms I had given to her, despite bringing the proverbial mountain to Mohammed approach, Mum was just not willing to climb; no matter my stance, she was not signing the forms!

I can still remember the look of shock, disbelief and then determination on Mrs. C____'s face. I am not sure if I asked her to speak to Mum, but that day, Mrs C____ came to see Mum. I took her upstairs to Mum's bedroom and when we went in, I remember Mum being in bed with the covers up to her eyes; it looked as she had really given up hope. Mrs C____ really spoke some Jamaican sense into Mum that day: "Sis, is what is wrong with you, man? Why you not signing de forms? You don't see your daughter is trying to help you? C'mon man, you have to sign the forms!"

It was the turning point; talk about light at the end of the tunnel! Short of saying "Lazarus come forth", Mum seemed to come to life and she promptly signed the form (well, not right there and then, but thankfully it was done within a very short space of time.!). That was all she had to do, because everything else had been completed and all that was needed was her moniker (now, if you know my Mum's name, you'll appreciate the word play; if not, it's an excuse for me to try and dazzle you with my literary knowledge!) I can laugh at the memory now, but believe me when I say I was not laughing then.

Having moved to a new GP, Mum was officially diagnosed as being severely disabled. When the forms were processed, Mum finally received the necessary benefits and entitlements to her just dues. For that, I say thank You, because it helped to ease the financial burden . . . just a little!

Over the years, I have watched my Mum struggle with her disability. To be fair, the borough's Social Services have been good, but watching my Mum at this new place in her life was yet another reminder of what and where *I* was; a middle-aged woman caring for an elderly parent. So imagine my reaction when the council fitted grab rails around the house for my Mum; yes, I was happy for her but on the other hand, I was mad! Why? Because it make everything about her condition and my role so . . . final, as if that was *my* lot. Forgive me if I seem a little selfish, but unless you have experienced this, it is quite hard to explain without appearing like a saint or an uncaring sinner . . . As mentioned before, I honestly felt I was aging before my time, which was why I was so angry! I wanted to rip them out and tear them down. I saw it as curtailing my love life (excuse me while I laugh at this point) because who wants to explain the pristine commode to potential "beaus"; it's hardly a passion-setter, is it? It was as if I didn't have much of a youth and now, here I was rapidly heading towards the autumn of life without having had much of a summer, just like a typical British weather scenario, eh!

Seriously though, I recognise there are many women in my position and I want to say the following to you: I understand. I truly understand. I understand the sighs and tight-lipped smiles when people congratulate you for what you are doing, when all you want is an opportunity to hand the reins of responsibility to someone else, for a night or two. I understand the long, painful glances at yourself in the mirror as you pass you by and feel that maybe life too, is rushing away . . . . I understand the pressure of having to carry you and your elderly parent(s) and the emotional strain of an inevitable role reversal. I understand when you have to make decisions for your parent(s) only to have them stubbornly refused and rebutted . . . and then have to face criticisms from those on the periphery of your pain asking you what are you doing and why don't you do this or that.

I understand the struggle in trying to define yourself: are you single or a carer? Does your parent(s) live with you—or you with them? Then there is the issue of relationships: how do you introduce or broach this aspect without looking for sympathy from a prospective "significant other"? And let's be honest: how many men are willing and able to take on a woman with parental responsibilities? It somehow makes you feel . . . vulnerable and exposed. Yes, for those sisters in similar circumstances, I understand.

I have heard some real horror stories about women who are caring for a parent (or parents) who are not appreciative, but are even more demanding of their children, as if it is somehow their daughters' fault (as they're the usual carers) as to why the parent is now where they are. Some parents are a deliberate drain on the emotions, mental faculties and finances. They require time, patience and effort it is not uncommon for childless children to have to struggle not to see their parent as their "child", for as their parent regresses, so the child becomes the parent and roles are reversed.

There are parents who seem to deliberately "act up", so the child (or children) is not able to live their own lives; it is as if the parent, having lived his/her life now wants the lives of their child as well! Some parents descend into places in the mind and spirit where the child can not follow and with sorrow, they sit outside watching longingly for a glimmer of recognition from one who once knew her every move, her every breath, her every cry. When dementia sets in and the recognisable becomes unfamiliar, the pain it causes is practically unbearable. You become a stranger and yet you have to hear your parent asking you for his/her daughter or son. It is not an easy road. And if you are single and are in this situation, it may seem as if that is all your life, as if that is all you have become, as if it's all that is left for you.

My sister, I want to encourage you . . . as I myself have been encouraged. There is an ancient promise, embedded in a rather unlikely place, which needs to be resurrected. In an ancient Law, it says "Honour your mother and father that your days may be long in the land which the LORD your God gives you". This is a promise of longevity when you step up to the mark and "honour" your parents. It may seem as if it will never end, as if your life is on hold, as if the rest of the world is passing you by while you're still stuck at first base, but rest assured, the Word is faithful; God never lies. What He has promised will and must surely come to pass, especially the promise of an abundant life in Him.

So, to my "caring sistas", as you continue to care for others, I encourage you to care for *yourself*, for the golden rule says you must "love others as you love yourself", As you enjoy life's open-top sandwich, make sure to include a topping you too can also enjoy. Rest and take time to stop. Book a holiday, a weekend break, a day trip—or a little retail therapy—but plan something just for *you*. Because when (not if, but *when*) your change comes, you will want to '*know you*' before you take the next step to another phase and another change on your journey. So to all those who are part of the open-top sandwich generation, be assured as you too "walk alone with One", for you are not on your own.

CHAPTER 4

Carnal Carnival

My journey took a definite change of direction when in 1985 I went to the Notting Hill Gate annual carnival with . . . my Mum. Don't laugh, it's true! At the time, most of the church crew I had grown up with had either left or were leaving the confines of church life and all that it pertained too. They had boyfriends, were dating, wearing real make-up and ear-rings (the latter was a real biggie for me, let me tell you). Yep, in my eyes, they were living life larger, better and beyond my wildest dreams. They were testing and experiencing life while I, like Rapunzel was just waiting for a chance and a change to let my hair down. My friends had gone by themselves and I was not allowed to go with them—at the tender young and vulnerable age of twenty (don't laugh!). I remember ringing a friend of mine, but she was going with J___, another family friend but someone whose clutches and control I was beginning to escape from and anyway, I really did not want to impose myself on them. 9When you are an only child, you are very much aware of the truth of the saying: "two's company but three's a crowd".)

So on that Bank Holiday I was home, moody, bored and vexed whilst the August sunshine was outside calling me. My Mum recognised the symptoms—let's face it, it was pretty hard to ignore the pout and woe-is-me look on my face—and offered to go with me. Now let's face it; can you imagine going to carnival with your Mum at the age of 20?!!? But realising the truth of the saying that "some is better than none" and muttered warnings from Mum to stay close we set out in the early afternoon to hit the carnival trail. When we finally reached what was to me a magical wonderland; I can still remember the call of the whistles in tune with the beat, the smoky aromas from dozens of food stalls, each one whetting my appetite and tantalising my taste buds; there was the pull of pulsating carnival currents as wave after wave of calypso, reggae and soca rhythms beat around and on me as pan, man and jam took hold of my senses.

Journey Pause: *With hindsight, can I really be blamed for what was to come as, coming from Trini parents, my cultural heritage is essentially roti, soca, mauby and "ting". I have often wondered where I got the inherent desire from to just "jump, wine and get on", as my Mum was never one for partying and the like. One reflection, maybe it was because, as an only child, I grew up quite sheltered. Mum only had one lamb and believe me when I say she was not going to let me become some man's lamb chop or curried mutton for anyone! So being someone who had never "raved" or partied in my teens—and a friend's 19th birthday house party and church youth socials really do not count. My growing years were spent in the safe confines of church and on reflection, I really do not mind, as it helped to fuel and develop a deep love for God from way back then. Indeed, when Mum had to go to work and I was invariably left on my own, my entertainment would be to "preach" to an imaginary audience of thousands as well as be the choir director, lead singer—and collect the offering! Yes, I had a great imagination as a child, but I used to really enjoy those times of the "Church of the One Soul"—me!*

So with that background, you can imagine my reaction when I took full advantage of the event to catch "ah wine on someting'", even though I was being heavily chaperoned at the time. In hindsight, I can only imagine my Mum's angst at what was happening around her and her whispered warning of "Shalisa, stay close by me, you hear", was somehow drowned out by the carnival beat. I never knew I could move like that—but I made sure to drop the moves only when Mum was distracted and not looking. We walked through the prescribed carnival route (back then it was bigger and better) with Mum asking me what I wanted to eat or drink and which stall looked better, only for me to hear one of Mum's derisive comments of " . . . huh, you call this carnival, all this jumping and getting on? In my day, carnival was carnival, decent! You didn't see people getting on like that!". Good thing she never knew that to "get on" was just what I wanted; a chance, just a little opportunity to "get on like that" too! It is at times like that that I warn people to be careful what you wish for . . . . !

On arrival, we bumped into some good ol' 'Tist souls—maybe they were out doing their own brand of street witnessing, I really don't know, but I recall feeling somewhat piqued that Mum was my carnival partner; not good for one's street cred, trust me. Not that I had much anyway, but I was mindful of the tiny bit I was trying to create.

Well, on that eventful day, we met a Trini float I recalled from the previous year. I persuaded Mum to follow it stressing the fact that it was Trini and therefore possibly more authentic than the others. The fact there were some serious movements going on around it might have had a little something to do with my desiring to go with it, but one just can't seem to remember . . . ! Then I met him ~ Mr. D. Hmmm, he made me feel like quick silver on golden sand as we moved together and I thought it was love. Mum was not so taken with his charms however, and I think that's when the time portals opened. Have you ever looked back at your life and been able to pin point where and when "it" all began? For me, on this leg of the journey, it was here. When that man held me, I found my Daddy; I was free from molestation; I was beautiful, slim and desirable.

When Mum's voice of reason broke through my dance-dazed mind to call me to go with her, my response, on reflection, was my first, fumbling effort to cut the invisible umbilical cord. It was a split-second decision ; to go to my life of singing along in my make-believe church with its congregation of one, or to remain in my actual church with no prospect of meeting boys (because the drought had started to kick in from back then as the "man shortage" famine was fast affecting the church) and even if they were there, to meet them was a serious no-no . . . Or should I sample the delights of carnival, step out and do something new for once? To move beyond watching to doing and being? I wanted to taste and see and to prolong the illusion, because I really didn't want the dream to end.

When the float moved forward, I remember Mum was there and I believed I reasoned that, if I moved just a few feet for a last "pan, man, jam" session, she would still be there. But when I (finally) looked back, she wasn't there. (As I write this, I think of all those times when we're faced with situations that, with hindsight we realise were instrumental in bringing us forward—or taking us back; of those events and decisions that have determined where we are now. That was a crossroads in my life and because of it, I am where and who I am now . . . .) I think I tried to make out I was shocked but at the time, I was too enthralled with and by Mr. D, who had me in the palm of his hand, his arms and his legs. Seems the time portals also opened for him too because he ended up "losing" his carnival friends as well.

This was exciting! At last life was beginning to happen for and to me! I was living and tasting life—what more could a NHS-bespectacled, chubby, insecure and introvert 20-year old want? Freedom's road was mine and I was not about to step off. In reminiscing, I think it is quite sad that carnival represented so much to me at the time . . .

Mr D. spoke to me, whispered compliments in my ear and I opened up like a new-born rose bud at the first touch of a summer's sun. How was he to know that my self esteem was rock bottom; no, tell a lie, it was non-existent? How could he know that his words were a lifeline to a young, black church girl, who had been molested a few years ago and who felt that her life was nothing, worthless, meaningless? How did he know that his whisperings had begun to shut out the "yes, you want it; you know you want it" that my molester had spoken into my very being?

I remember thinking that, although we had lost our respective chaperones and friends, we had each other. We made a pretence of looking for my Mum, just to say we were doing something and tried to appear duly concerned about it all, but surprise, surprise, we didn't find her—instead we found each other. Never mind my predicament about losing Mum wondering how I'd get home—man, I was having the time of my life! This was living and much better than standing in my living room and singing out of the hymn book to an imaginary crowd! Oh Lord, I had found life! A man, a real live, bonafide man (trust me on that one!) was interested in me, ME! He was not ashamed to be seen with me, ME! Why, he even held my hands in public and kissed me . . . in public!

Now, if you're rather squeamish, you may wish to turn over at this point. You see, I had never really been kissed up until then. I was still a virgin at 20 years old and my first "proper" kiss was by a good friend of mine when I as 18. That was it . . . until Mr. D. You never forget those moments.

When his lips touched mine, there was nothing like it! It was better than Mum's rice & peas, curry and roti AND black cake in one sitting! Lips have always held a fascination for me and boy, his lips had it all. Not too large, too small, too thin or too full—they were just right. Not too much or too little tongue but just enough to tantalise and get me wanting and needing more. (He later said he realised I was a beginner, so was very gentle with me . . .)

We touched, kissed, touched and kissed . . . at Notting Hill Carnival . . . in broad daylight. It was only when we heard remarks from other carnival-goers that we realised we might be going too far; for unlike today, it was still the mid-eighties and those things were usually done behind closed doors in a private setting. But I didn't care. I was in love. It was destiny. The portals were opened and could never be closed. I didn't know the man. I only knew that when he held me in his arms I had found my Daddy. I was accepted by the human race. I could fit in. I was special. I was clean and pure. I was beautiful.

I remember Mr D's laugh when he heard the comments and remarks about our behaviour; like him, it was slow, quiet and intimate and resonated within me. He simply held me even closer and whispered " . . . let's find somewhere quieter". Thrills went down my virgin body to know that this gorgeous, brown-skinned Jamaican man actually wanted to go somewhere quiet with me, me! Wow!

By around 10pm, I guess we finally and silently agreed to quit all pretence of looking and searching for his friends and my Mum, as we realised they were long gone—and we didn't have a glimmer of a chance of even beginning to know where to look . . . not that we wanted too, of course. By then, we'd stop kissing long enough to actually talk and we realised we lived in completely opposite directions; we had no money between us apart from a few pounds (remember, I was still very much reliant on the "Bank of Mum") and of course, there were no mobile phones and very few ATMs (how on earth did we ever survive in those days, I wonder!)

But Mr. D continued to introduce me to myself that evening. We found another solitary area, on a house step, one where the street-light was candle-light in the trees and there, he kissed my face, my neck, my ears ohh, so tenderly and lovingly. I just knew he was "heaven sent" as he knew where, when and how to go. It was only when we realised the intensity of our desire, situation—and position—that we managed to gather ourselves before the owners came home. I'm sure that if they'd arrived a few seconds later, we'd have been arrested for indecency. Mr D. awoke some things in me that night: passion and desire, sexuality and sensuality. When I reflect on my "awakening", I believe Mr. D saw past the NHS glasses, the unfashionable clothes, the spots and pimples of a gawky, shy and immature girl-woman to the real me that was reaching out, looking for acceptance and affirmation . . . and the love of a daddy long gone . . .

An hour later, just after 11pm, whether by accident or cosmic design, we managed to reach the rendezvous he'd previously arranged with his friends—but of course, they were not there. It was then that the cobweb-like touch of panic drifted past my now heightened senses and began to tug at my rational mind as the realisation hit me: how was I ever going to get home? As reason began to return like a dog who'd been turned out for bad behaviour and was now looking to make amends, I was shocked by my own behaviour and felt a deep sense of shame as I began to think about how and what my Mum was going through. Yet, strangely, this was a new thing for me as I'd experienced an awakening and had, in some bizarre way, achieved my "aim"—hadn't I?

By this time, we were so tired, our feet were killing us but when you get a taste for something, you just don't let something as mundane as a few blisters stop you. We went to where some street cleaners were beginning the carnival clean up, somewhere near Grove Station, I think. We found a bench and sat down and he pulled me onto his lap; me, "10-Ton Tessie", or so I had often been called. I nervously jumped up and tried to explain that, due to my excessive weight and obesity, I didn't like to sit any one's (man's) lap.

Journey pause: *looking back, I was never as big as I thought or made myself out to be. But you know how downright mean and cruel kids can be and when you don't have father, sister or brother to fight your corner and cover your back, you just accept your lot in life as the butt of* *everyone's "fat jokes". I mean, I was usually the benchmark, the litmus test for others when they were describing or assessing size: "Well, she was almost as big (or a little smaller) than Shalisa" or "he was almost twice the size of Shalisa but taller". A family friend, usually took great delight in repeating the, oh-so-old-and-tired anecdote of how I nearly killed someone playing "leap frog" at a social sports' event; yep, I was the fat one, the ugly one, the clown one. Coming from such a background, you can imagine, I was usually the last to be picked for sports and social events and the first to be the punch line for so many jokes. So don't judge me too harshly for what I did . . . please.*

Back to Mr. D. He pulled me back onto his lap and (thankfully) survived to tell the tale and I remember just melting into him. He laid his head on my bosom and I remember the pleasure I gained in just stroking and caressing his face. His eyes, nose and lips, oh, those lips . . . every contour of his face was mine that night. When we finally managed to stand up and come to ourselves once, we found we had an audience—again. (Hmmm, maybe, there's a deep seated voyeuristic streak in me somewhere . . .). By now, it was way past midnight and all thoughts of going home had disappeared from my mind; the heat of the moment had dissolved all reason, warning and sensibility. Mr D. was also resigned to our fate to think about family, loved ones and responsibility. We were too busy enjoying the twilight zone, that place where dreams and desires do come true, where the "real" persona can dare to come out. Yes, we were each other's stars in the twilight zone that night.

1.30am. Reason and the cold London night air really started to kick in as, induced by the cold and fuelled by sheer tiredness and hunger, we began discussing some really crazy plans on how to get to our respective homes. The most sensible one involved us taking a cab to from West London to my home outside London and then Mr D. would take it to his home on the other side of town. When I raised the minor issue of how we were going to pay, he said he would do a runner. The fact the cabbie could well return to my home or phone the police did not cross our minds. Thankfully, there were no cabs available, thus giving us more time to enjoy our own personal carnival procession. It was then that we spied a chicken shop still open, where a group of 15 or so people were waiting for their return coach to Birmingham. But, even in the face of such adversity, we held hands and enjoyed the spicy fried chicken aroma, as we enjoyed the "lurve" that had brought us together. It's funny how such minor details seem to stay forever engraved in your memory . . . .

Journey Pause: *In my journal, I'd recorded that ". . . it was nice having a guy to hold me and caress me and vice versa; it felt good to hold a real, live man and imagine him as mine (*Journal entry, Tuesday 27th August 1985!*) ". So when I talk about the "twilight zone", I'm talking about how a need or a desire can make you think, feel and believe an illusion is real. That was where I was. When I look back on that time, I wish I could go back to meet me; I'd just hug me and tell me to let it go—it's not real and I should begin to love myself. But then, would I have really listened? Probably not because I was coming from a position of need where to me, half a loaf was better than none and even crumbs were a better alternative to starvation. Why am I going into so much depth regarding this phase of my journey? Because one's sexual awakening is indeed a milestone. How, when, where and with whom it happens can and does shape and impact you—and if it's a negative relationship, one of abuse, violence, etc, even if you bury it deep in the recesses of the mind, it will surface in your relationships with others—and yourself. You see, in a strange yet understanding way, every time Mr. D held me during that night, I'd close my eyes and imagine it was my Daddy holding me and telling me that he really loved and cared for me. The memory was enough to make me forget unwanted and painful fumblings and bitter words which had recently lost their sting . . .*

But who said God doesn't have a sense of humour, for even there, I really believe God was making sure I did not and could not forget who and Whose I was, even though the path I was on was not good at all. At around 3am, S_____ came into the shop; he was from a South London church and I knew him from having seen him at various youth and church programmes. In the midst of my golden haze, I just heard "Shalisa? Shalisa? Is you gal?" Talk about coming back to earth with a bump! I gasped out his name in shock, (whereas before I'd been whispering "Mr D, Mr. D!") and sat up straight! But that was the extent of our conversation and when he left, he looked at me as if to say "you go, girl!" What a validation! I felt I was now "acceptable"; that I had now gotten my permit to be officially seen in public with a wonderful example of all-black masculinity. Okay, on reflection, maybe I am slightly exaggerating Mr D's overall appearance—but I am sure there's a woman (or two) out there who's sagely nodding her head and sighing, because she realises that hey, she's not the only one to see life through rose-coloured glasses . . .

Believe it or not, Mr D and I managed to speak in-depth that night; my first time of really speaking one-on-one with a man of my desires—in the flesh and not just a figment of my imagination! But then the bombshell came: Mr. D told me he had a girlfriend and a new baby. At the time, I thought his admission was a sign of honesty and that he really appreciated me. Little did I know it then, but my decision to continue seeing him—even though I knew what I knew—was to set a painful and precarious precedent for my life. I didn't realise it, but my decision was my first step on the generational path established by my father, years before. You see, my father had set the pattern for me by having several children by several women—two of them in the same year and same month! (But more about that later . . . !).

I had often wondered what I had inherited from my Dad and, in retrospect, I believe it was a desire of and for the flesh. He loved women and I loved men, plain and simple as that and my carnival experience was my initiation on a path I was yet to discover, but which seemed to have been mapped out for me. Out of all my sisters, I believe I am the only one like this, because when I review my journals (or life chronicles as I also like to term them), the path taken is clearly seen.

Journey Pause: *Now, I thank God for having taken that mentality away. He has shown and taught me what it is to live a clean life, to honour myself and above all, He has shown me the reality of a Father's love. The love I had always been seeking was what He always had for me. It must have truly grieved and hurt His heart to see me looking in the garbage bags of life for nourishment when He had already prepared an exquisite banqueting table of love for me to partake of and enjoy. Thank you, Lord; it wasn't and indeed is not always easy but here I am today and for that, I have to say "Thank You."*

When I got home, it was to face the reality and pain of a newly cut umbilical cord. For me, it was my first taste of freedom, but for Mum,

I guess it was the first piercing pain of having to let go. How did I get home? Good ol' night bus! Dawn had already risen and the birds were well into their third round of their "dawn chorus" when I walked up the stairs, unlocked the door and went inside to face my Mum. I knew she had to have been in shock because she didn't even shout at me; in fact, it would have been better if she had ranted and taken her fear and hurt out on me but no, she spoke in a small, little voice. I did not feel good or mature at all; rather like the naughty child I was. Years later, she told me that she went through so many emotions, ranging from anger to rage to a cold, numbing despair as she began to imagine and to live and re-live in her imagination the worst possible scenarios, whilst all the time I was canoodling and carrying on my own carnival with Mr D. Seems she had an all-night prayer vigil for her only child. Little did we know that that night heralded the first baby steps on my journey of walking alone . . . with One. I recall Mum crying and me trying to explain a situation I'd never been in before and feelings I'd never experienced before.

But why, do you ask, was I so desperate to escape? Why was I looking to get away from my circumstances? At the time of writing my journey experiences, as I'd mentioned before, my Mum lives with me. Whilst I know I love her dearly, I realise my relationships were not only looking for a father's love, but also reflected my efforts to escape "Mommy dearest!". Now, for those who know me, I know that sounds really strange and out of character, but please—give me a moment to explain . . . There was, is, a need within that I have to acknowledge, because stifling it and trying to pretend it doesn't exist has caused me to do some things that, on reflection, are wrong. I recognise the need to honour myself and the best way to do that, is to take this opportunity to be truthful with myself. My "carnal carnival" experience was my timid efforts and tentative steps into adulthood, away from the protective confines of religion and church and all that pertained to it. I was stepping out to be someone, to be somebody . . . If only I knew where my steps would lead me.

The following day, Mr. D rang me at 10.40am at work (yep, I noted the exact time in my journal.!) and so my journey continued. We arranged to meet and I could hardly focus that day; I think I must have lost 8lbs instantly with nerves and anticipation! You see, its one thing to get caught up in the moment but it's another to have to meet the moment that you got caught up in, ha ha! He met me at my work place and I still recall the butterflies and heightened sense of anticipation and desire just knowing he was on his way.

When the front desk announced a "Mr. D is here to see Shalisa", I nearly passed out! Trust me, I had it baaad for Mr D! When I saw him, all the feelings, passion and desire rushed back. We crossed the road to Green Park which for a long time during our "relationship", was the repository of some very fond, tender and passionate memories as I enjoyed and explored the sensation of "being in love". In retrospect, I was living in a fool's paradise, because as we all know, all that glitters is not gold or the real McCoy. Yet naivety is an eager yet blind student, always willing to accept what a more mature and experienced scholar in the school of life would immediately recognise as a fake and an illusion.

But Mr D was there for me, the new, emerging me, and our days became weeks and then months of personal, sexual and emotional discovery. He was my "first" intimate experience and that is why I can now understand advice of not giving yourself too soon to so many, because you end up with numerous soul ties and a deeply scarred heart. Thus the scene was set and the route programmed into my emotional and relational GPS, as over the years, I found myself limping from one relationship to another, becoming entangled, always trying to score that first euphoric high from yet another "hit"—only to realise that in most of the relationships I was never *his* number one or even the *only* one but just another easy and gullible lay.

Journey Pause: *In remembering and reflecting, I can see how time has healed me. Whereas before, the bitter bile of the past would rise up to choke and remind me, now I can reflect with a bittersweet remembrance on a part of my life that has helped to shape me and bring me to where I now am. Dear reader, what about you? What memories have you locked away that are too painful to mention much less to bring out in the open, even to discuss with yourself? Just be thankful that where you once were you are there no longer and if you are there, don't be afraid to step out and change the direction of your walk. It's all up to you . . . .*

So what happened to Mr. D, I hear you ask? Well, thanks to the wonders of modern technology and the growth of social online networks, he contacted me via a well-known site. Can you imagine what it felt like to hear from your "first love" after some 20-odd years? At the time, I was nursing (yet!) another broken heart when "ping", I got his message. When I saw his name come up on the "incoming-mail" alert, I was instantly transported back to Notting Hill carnival to the exact same time and place, and could practically taste the atmosphere and hear the sounds from our first meeting. Everything, the sights, sounds, and adrenaline just came flooding back, like an out-of-body experience, as long-forgotten and buried emotions, feelings and sensations rushed to the forefront, pushing aside the mediocrity of the here and now.

As I read and re-read his message (now tell the truth—you'd do the same thing too!), I realised where he had left me was not where he now found me. I was no longer where I used to be. I had changed. My walk, my focus and priorities had all changed and were not what they used to be. Indeed, the motivation, issues and pressures I now faced were all different—and so were my responses and coping mechanisms to what life was throwing at; I just didn't respond the same way, any more. You know, it is truly amazing how a letter, an email, a call or even a text message can just take you right back to what you thought was long forgotten and long gone. But before you ask, let me just share with you what he had to say:

> *"Shalisa, when I think of you I don't have any regrets. You were there when I needed you, like every man needs a woman. I travelled far to reach your destination and you have always been a good friend to me. Do you think we can meet up some time? I remain your friend, as always, Mr. D".*

I cried when I read his message, because I remembered . . . not just the passion and the bittersweet awakening of losing myself to find the new me, but I remembered the talks we shared, the intimate, personal and intricate discussions about life, love . . . and God. I had often longed for that special connection to that special someone, to be able to openly and honestly discuss the deep things of life. It's strange, but in the midst of the madness, the uncertainty, the emotional rollercoaster of stepping into "big people business" in my first ever relationship, knowing deep within that what we, I, was doing was wrong, I somehow and in someway, always sought to share and open up to him about my love and desire for God! An example of this is noted in the following journal entry:

> *I'm praying for Mr. D. I regret the way we said good-bye. I wanted to tell him of God's love and how God is waiting for him to love Him back in return" (October 1987!)*

Fast forward some 15 or so years later. When life was beginning to catch up with and overtake me, I made a conscientious decision to honestly admit, acknowledge and seek to deal with my soul-ties from previous relationships. Facing up to and uncovering each and every one of them was a deeply personal and sometimes bitter exercise. It was one of life's epiphany moments, where I had to face myself, my reality and to see it for what it was. I could no longer pretend to have been the victim in so many sad and sordid relationships (none of which are would be deemed outside the norm by today's standards). It was hard to look into the mirror of one's self and see, really see who and what I was—just broken. I remember praying for help to God to help me cancel out any negative repercussions of *my* behaviour, *my* actions, *my* input and for my exes to only remember the good I might have said about Him. I especially asked for forgiveness for being the proverbial church gal hypocrite, because I was not a good "PR" agent. For Mr. D, I silently prayed that he would remember the good and forgets the bad, because I truly believe God is more than able to bring peace and calm out of life's chaos and perplexities . . .

Journey Pause: *What are soul-ties, I hear you ask. In essence, these tend to arise from sexual intimacies, but can equally stem from an emotional tie you have forged with someone at a deeper level, where you allow someone to enter not just your body but your mind, heart and soul. "Soul ties" are why you can't forget "Fred" after all these years, even though you've since moved on, married, had children, eloped, migrated, changed your hairstyle, had a tummy tuck and/or a face lift. In other words, a "soul tie" is when his face comes back at the most unexplained times, even during those intimate moments. It is evoked at the hint of a certain aftershave, the sound of a certain song, the words someone may say, albeit innocently, which serve to evoke dormant memories. It is the reason why you can't find fulfilment with your current partner/spouse* *because "Fred" is still there, inside your mind and inside of you, the secret you. And it's here, in your secret place, where, whether known or unknown to your own self, he continues to hold sway over you and refuses to let you go, often because you don't want to be let go.*

So what happened? Wouldn't it be funny if, after all of the above, I decided to see him. Don't think I wasn't tempted because when you've lit a fire before, you sure don't forget how to get it going again the second time. No, my response to Mr. D's invitation to take a walk down memory lane was a case of "thanks, but no thanks". Although Mr. D was an integral part of my journey, the woman I was then is not the woman I am now. I am no longer the same. I realised I have walked too far on my journey to turn back now . . . but I did welcome the moment to take the time to pause, stop and reflect and walk this road with you before we move on to another journey milestone . . . .

❋

═══════════════════════════════

CHAPTER 5
───────────────────────────────

Ol' Chocolate

*On reviewing my journal journeys thus far, I am at some of the events I have walked through—experiences and incidences I dread to think about facing now, let alone go through! On reading the following journal entry I felt I had to include it, because, after close reflection, it helped me realise and confirm that yes, we are all here for a reason. I'm sure there are many women who have gone through similar experiences and have dismissed it at nothing of any consequence, but if you would allow yourself to take a moment to step back, be still and reflect, you would realise that yes, there **was** more to the experience than you had thought. For if only one thing had happened differently, how vast should, would and could have been the difference and your current destination. So let me gently guide you through as I revisit this journey pathway—for I'm sure there's something here for you . . .*

"So much has happened since I was last here! I tried to kill myself on 30th May 1988. Praise God I failed. Why did I try? Because I'd gotten "involved" with a guy (yet again!) called A.A. We nearly had sex. I walked home from (his house) in Islington at 1.00am. God provided a taxi for me—He cares".
5th June 1988:

Let me just take a moment to elaborate and give the background to what was going on. I was tired of living. At 23 years, I had grown tired and weary of trying to make God love me or a man love me, much less trying to find something to love about myself. Oh, and let's not forget, having never been able to get a Father's love, I unconsciously still felt the need to keep on trying, hence the mindless, emotional and relational merry-go-round that I was on. Because of the nothingness I was feeling and the fact there was no one to turn to or confide in; because I felt that, although the situation was not of my own making, I had somehow become my own assassin, suicide seemed the only way out and so it was that I took the obligatory tablets. I guess that the fact I'm writing my story is a good indication I didn't make it but I did wake up with a serious headache the next day—and a sense of relief, because I realised it was not only a coward's way out, but the pain I would cause those who loved me was not worth it.

Now Mr. A was the first of many relationships I had with "brothas" from the "fatherland" (aka Africa!). Back then, it was all about originality and what I considered to be the "real McCoy", which for me meant, tall, dark (literally!) and handsome—I guess two out of three was a good enough bet! The "fatherland brothas" seemed to ooze an air of confidence and self-awareness that I appealing and endearing. The ones I found—or who found me—came with a pervading air of masculinity—which I later discovered was, for some, a thin covering for selfish arrogance and manipulation—but then, they had it goin' on! However, to a young, naïve and impressionable 20-something, Mr A was old enough to be my father—and I believe that was the pulling factor! He was what I thought I looking for—maturity, stability, responsibility; someone to simply notice and look after the little girl inside of me. Little did I know emotional myopia was causing me to see what was not really there.

I met Mr. A on a trip to Carnaby Street. I'd just finished an exam and felt like wanting to relieve the swinging Sixties, only I didn't realise they'd already swung by, and, in an effort to be grown up, decadent and retro chic, I went to Carnaby Street. Never mind I was a couple of decades out of date. At that time, I was trying to excel educationally and my preferred route was part-time study, especially when it afforded me great opportunities to enjoy the sights and sounds of good ol' London. I strolled down Carnaby Street trying to capture the feel of the place, and it felt great! The sun was shining and I was enjoying the moment. Little did I know what was literally around the corner . . . .

When Mr. A approached me, I was stunned and completely overwhelmed this tall, gorgeous, smooth-skinned, chocolate drop, with a glistening moustache and a crown of curly, soft, touchable hair, tinged at the temples with a hint of silver, would even notice yet alone approach me. He stopped me and asked for directions (okay, I told you was I was very naïve and didn't realise it was a chat up line!). He then introduced himself in very soft yet assertive modulated tones. When he told me he had studied at Oxford University and you know I believed him because his plumy accent seemed so authentic. Wow, this was a dream come true; Prince Charming was indeed alive and well! My introduction to the "finer things of life" was the sip of first ever cappuccino in my first ever Italian coffee bar and boy, was I living life in the fast lane! He engaged my eyes and my mind as we sat and sipped and I kept pinching myself as to how I was in this fantastic place with such a sophisticated man. He was "suited and booted" and was with little ol' me. He seemed to take a genuine interest, asking where I was from, where I was going and what I was doing in between. Being so very worldly-naïve, I naturally opened up (because who doesn't like attention) about who I was, where I was from, the course I was doing, and on and on. I talked, he listened and offered suggestions and advice on what and where my life could go. To me, he was the "father figure" I'd been subconsciously seeking—and I wasn't about to lose my father the second time around . . .

It's strange, but when I recalled this memory, I simply can't remember how we ended up at his house, the journey from Carnaby Street to where he lived, the conversation nor even the mode of transport. No, the next razor-sharp recollection is being in his bed, naked, wondering what and how the hell did I get there? What *was* I doing here? Have you ever felt shame but been unable to cover up? Well that was me, when I realised I was where I knew I shouldn't be. Yet some strange reason, I do remember him telling me how a man from his country can tell how old a girl is when making love to her—and yes, you guessed it; I believed him! Talk about being naïve to the max!

Journey Pause: *When a man like that holds, kisses and caresses you, you think the world is your oyster and you are its pearl! Yet when you mistake physical expressions as a desire to fill a deep seated emotional* *need, you realise the factors don't all add up to a perfect equation. Naivety is no respecter of colour, creed, race or age; it'll sneak up on you at whatever stage you are in and hit you right between the eyes. Sadly, it's only when you've been attacked time and time again that you learn to put up the electric-wired fencing, only to wonder why no one is getting through and nor are you able to get out.*

Well that night, we tried or rather, he tried to "gauge my age" and even though my body was physically ready, my mind was still so very confused and trying to decipher where and what was going on. Thankfully, after several painful attempts, he opted to at least try to penetrate my mind. It is so amazing what you can take in when in a vulnerable and exposed place and position. Even though I'd have probably dismissed what he was saying at any other time, in that moment it effectively seemed to "hook" me into him, as it was very encouraging when someone of such an assumed calibre speaks with authority into your life. In a rather bizarre way he was not wrong, for he told me I should go back to college and university, because I had " . . . a lot of talent and purpose" and so on. I heard him but did not and could not listen to the advice given not only because of my vulnerable position, but because I had now begun to be concerned with how I was going to get home from North London to Essex, at that time in the morning?

In the midst of his unorthodox careers' advice as he continued to speak, the reality began to nudge and kick in and I slowly, somehow managed to get up and out of the bed. I remember getting dressed (it always seems to be in slow motion) and getting ready to leave, because I had always maintained I would never sleep over at a man's house. I mean, it was something that "good girls" just didn't do . . . and to do so would mean I was really not walking right, especially as I was a "church girl". Isn't it amazing how we can delude ourselves to the point where we begin to think that wrong is right and right is gone? Where we can interpret the words and actions of others to suit ourselves in an effort to give credibility to our own actions? Suddenly, Mr. A's chocolate attraction no longer seemed so sweet or so appealing; I'd gorged myself and was now starting to feel sick,

When I was reading the original journal entry, I had to ask myself—what kind of man would let a young girl walk home alone—in the dark—at that time of night? Truth be told, I guess the series of events—one cappuccino and I'm in bed with him—was not a positive portrayal of myself.

When I left his house and stepped through the door onto the pavement, it was 1.30am and I was about to walk on a very dark, tree-lined road at night, in the dark. Darkness of night, body and soul and it was cold, very cold but I had stubborn pride to keep me warm. I walked to the end of the road and when I got to the junction, I just stood there. I did not have a clue where I was much less how to get to where I was going. The roads were lonely and desolate and thankfully, I was fortunate not to have any unpleasant encounters—but it wasn't because of any worldly wisdom on my part. I remember taking a turn somewhere, somehow, in some direction which seemed to have more street lights, which I took for a good sign and then just walking, walking, walking, trying to keep warm and safe and above all, not to think. I just couldn't believe I'd just had a one-night stand! Me!

Journey Pause: *In my mind at that time, it just made more sense to walk where there was more light than to try to brave the unknown in a darker environment. I was glad for the darkness, the cold and the bleakness of where I was, as it matched how I was feeling and experiencing. When I review my life thus far, it has made sense for me to wish I had stuck to the light on my journey! There have been times when I have looked at the light but instead chose to go the other way and have lived to regret it. Truly, it is the mercies of God why I am still here . . .*

After some time, during which I had resigned myself to having to walk home, I was approached by two black girls who asked me for directions. Talk about irony, for it was a case of the blind asking the can't see! I said I didn't live in the area and wasn't sure of what or where anything was, as I too was trying to get home. I don't know what else I told them but boy, was I glad for the company! They said lived in Stratford and, as they were looking to take a cab, they offered to take me that far. Now, I had no money on me to pay for a cab from wherever the hell I was, but I figured I could at least get a night bus or something from Stratford to my home in Ilford. (Ever notice how when we're in tight spots and painful predicaments we often try to plea-bargain and barter with ourselves?) Thankfully, we managed to find a cab firm in the area and thankfully, were able to get a cab. I sat in the car as if in a dream because surely, this was not happening to me, but sadly, the cold night air was a constant reminder of where I was.

When they got home, they asked the cab driver to wait a while. They went inside and then returned with £10 for me to be able to continue the rest of the journey. I never got their names, I don't know their names, but in reliving and sharing this memory, I publicly wish to thank God for loving and helping me through their love and generosity. Over the years, whenever I have walked down this particular memory lane, I've always asked God to bless them for their act of kindness to a total stranger.

When the cab pulled into the estate, and I had finally reached home, I realised the fare was £4 or £5 more than anticipated! What to do? It's at those times you realise there's no place like home and no one like Mum—yes the same place and person I was trying to flee the nest from.

I ran upstairs and said "Mum—don't ask me any questions; please not now, but do you have any money to pay for a cab please? Don't ask any questions, please, don't ask!" And love-in-action did just that; Mum gave me the necessary change and I don't recall her asking any questions. It was the next day that Mum shared how she felt her insides had been cut and dragged out with worry as she imagined every car pulling up, every faint knocking or distant call was the one she was dreading . . . .

Why am I sharing this? Because in writing and reviewing my life, I've obviously had time to stop, think, review and analyse the many twists and turns I've encountered thus far. As mentioned earlier, this is not a tale of sex, drugs and rock n roll, but I do believe it echoes and mirrors the experiences of many an "average" woman—with a unique tale of their own. That night could well have been my last as I was setting myself up for SO many things to happen to me. I really believe God sent or allowed those two girls to help me get home and once again, whoever and wherever you are, may there be others to help you along your own journeys whenever you may need it.

When I think back over that time, I was really so confused and unsure of myself, of life and even though I was a "good church gal" who "looked" like I was all-together and level-headed, yet deep, deep down, I was drowning in myself; I was struggling to know God (and to recognise if He even existed); I was struggling to get deeper with Him whilst trying to fight the devil, the world—and my natural, human desires. (It is only now I realise that hormones were actually created for a good and positive purpose; for at the time, I always felt I was fighting a losing battle with my inherent nature . . .)

It was only recently on reflecting about the incident with Ol' Chocolate, that I realised that hey, maybe, just maybe, my life had been preserved for something for a reason, a purpose. For it's only when I look back that I can see my journey was never solo; there was always Someone, somewhere in the wings, walking in the shadows, watching and overseeing me.

This is reflected in the following journal extract of **8 June 1988:**

> *God is good; I pray for His help so that I can cope . . . for when the heat is on, instead of spurring me onto higher things, I tend, instead, to wilt, droop and die.*

> *God's hand will and is guiding me*
> *Although the path be dark and grim*
> *Beset with the many pitfalls of sin*
> *Yet my hope is seared in Him*
> *Yes, I'm safely led.*

> *When temptations I cannot see*
> *Seem to wrestle and overcome me;*
> *My weak voice He doth heed*
> *For I am safely led.*

> *When despair held me fast*
> *Despondent, suicidal, I seek to breath my last*
> *Yet I am promised that this too comes to past*
> *For by my God I am safely led.*

And then that day I will see
Him who has loved me eternally
Then I will sing on glassy sea
"Praise my God, I was heavenly led!"

17th **July 1988**: I found this entry very telling . . .

I plan to get re-baptized this coming Sabbath. There've been many doubts, for, in the eyes of the majority, I've been in "good & regular standing". I prayed and tonight, after talking to the evangelist, I decided to go forward. This is no joke—but a serious move. No turning back—I want, nay, I NEED God to re-direct my life in the way He wants me to go. Pentecost is coming again & I do NOT want to be left out . . . I opened God's word—Isaiah 62:10-12: "Go through, go through the gates . . ." I will GO THRO THE GATES into life eternal".

11th **October 1988:**

Today, I leave my life an open book. For God is indeed able to work within me, above all that I ask Him for. Read Ephesians 3:20-21.

Dear Father, I ask for a closer walk with Thee,
For deeper faith, hope and charity;
For the strength Satan's darts to overcome
For the courage to hold on till You come.

Oh God! Without You my life is unreal
Empty my love—no touch, nothing can I feel;
This day sweep into me, a mighty flood
And let me then be filled with the Power of God.

So what ever happened to my "Ol' Chocolate"? Well, after a while I realized he was not the one for me (yes, it always takes a while for the penny to drop!). I was stupid enough to agree to meet him (ever notice how hurting people like to keep putting their hand back into the fire?). We'd meet and after a while I began to realize he was always a pound (or ten) short when we'd go out, which thankfully wasn't often as I noticed he was now trying to tap into the bank of "Shalisa", making withdrawals than deposits. It was an incident with my car that helped me to get over—and to get out!

I had asked him not to touch something, which he promptly ignored and the result meant the problem had to be fixed ASAP. I went to a friend of mine who, on seeing him in the car, pulled me to one side to ask me what I was doing with "Father Moses" (seems there was more grey in his hair and beard than I cared to remember!) My friend's remark was the proverbial eye opener. For what I thought was a distinguished, worldly-wise look on a fine mature brother was in reality, a greying old man, probably desperate to re-capture his long-lost youth and who was hoping I'd be his signpost.

So in closing, I have to remind you that, although a little chocolate can be good for you, remember to leave Ol' Chocolate alone.!

CHAPTER 6

The Move

The following extracts about "The Move" are based on my journal entries at the time as they best record the exhilaration and angst I went through, as well as all the other emotions in-between! Studies have shown that moving house is one of the most top five stressful situations for the majority of people and trust me, you had better believe it! For those planning to move home, I encourage you to read, ponder and reflect; for those who have gone through this traumatic experience, I am sure you will empathise! When reviewing aspects of my journey thus far, "The Move" ranks as one of the best things I've accomplished to date, but it certainly did not feel like it at the time. Believe me when I say it took YEARS for me get over and to recover from it! Anyway, read on to see how "The Move" was an integral part of my journey and how it could be an introduction to your own sense of relocation . . .

Background:

In the last spring of my life, around the tender age of 27 or 28, when it began to dawn on me that Prince Charming was either stuck in traffic, his sat nav/GPS was not working or he simply was not interested in coming to "take me away from all this" so I decided to take matters into my own hands. No way was I going to gather dust on the proverbial shelf—no way! I began to seriously think about the notion of being a home owner, of moving on and up. Yes, it was the mid 90's and being considered a BUPPIE was something to aspire too . . . and so the thought of actually moving from the council flat which had been home for most of my life, began to evolve and take shape. I was beginning to catch a glimpse of a rather unpleasant future: where living in a flat with no lift meant as Mum aged, getting out and about would be more difficult for her and consequently for me. I was seeking to escape what I saw as "the inevitable" and this galvanised me to get up and get going to see what I could be doing.

Journey Pause: *Let me just take a moment or two to define what I mean by "the inevitable". For me, "the inevitable" was me still being joined by an invisible umbilical cord to Mum, when all I wanted was to run free and wild (for those who remember, think "Born Free!") It was a sense of looking at my current situation as being an indicator of where I could end up, despite desperate yearnings steer towards a different conclusion. This was further compounded when all around me, friends and acquaintances seemed to be marrying, living together or at least "pairing up", having children and merging into their new homes, whilst all I could see was an unenviable sea of "sameness"—and it was **that** I was struggling to get away from. I had hoped, like many a woman out there, to have been "further along" in life (and that's a phrase I've heard quite often from other women along their own journey), but I didn't realise then that "the inevitable" was an integral part of my journey and to try to escape or to attempt to circumnavigate it would only serve to prolong the lesson that life was teaching me.*

However, the fact our flat had recently been flooded and had damaged those below us, could be deemed another all-important motivating factor as well! Grab a coffee, a couple of biscuits and let me tell you about it—what a day that was . . . .

It was a Saturday in May and we had planned to go to church and then onto a friend's house for fellowship lunch, something which was very much for the norm for us to do. At around 5.30/6.00am, I heard a frantic banging on the front door. Jumping up from a deep sleep (in which I thought I was being attacked by raging drum), I rang barefoot from by bedroom, wrenched open the living room door . . . and stepped into inches of ice cold water! Let me tell you, if I wasn't awake before, I was certainly awake then! I ran across the now sodden carpet, each ice-cold footstep reminding me this was definitely not a dream and when I got to the door, the long-suffering tenant from the ground floor simply said, somewhat apologetically, "Erm, so sorry to disturb you, but I think your flat might be flooded".

Now, don't you just hate it when someone spells out the obvious; tell me something I didn't know! Welcome to a classic lesson in the "Art of Understatement 101!" It seemed a pipe had burst in the kitchen and had flooded the kitchen and the front room and because water will always find a way, it then seeped through the empty flat below us, to the ground floor flat . . . which had just been decorated. In style. I mean, real expensive décor and style. The tenant even had a proper fireplace and wooden flooring, before such items were deemed fashionable and de rigueur.

So the seed of wanting to move on and out was I believe, born on that day and it continued to grow, especially when the carpet then started to dry out and leave it's own peculiar fragrance . . . oh yes, it was really time to move on up and out of there!

Journey Pause: *Isn't it awful when certain events, even if not of your own making, will insist on lingering to remind you of what had happened? They make sure you can not and will not forget they happened because they then start to stink! Like most things, we thought we could do some damage control, suck up most of the water and let it dry out naturally but life does not always co-operate so easily, does it! I mean, it was only a little mistake, not even our fault but, oh boy, did it leave an unpleasant fragrance. Not wanting to spoil the taste of your coffee and dunking biscuit, just take a moment to stop, reflect and do a "sniff" test for anything that could be alerting you to the fact that you might need to get rid of some things in order to clear the air—and possibly your heart . . .*

At this juncture, I really should explain I am not very good at asking for things. Don't get me wrong, I will if I have to, but by then life had taught me that asking puts you at the mercy of the person being asked who, if they want to be sheer bloody-minded could say "no" just for the sake of saying "no". However, at the time, a positive bonus of Thatcherism enabled council tenants to take up the offered the option of either buying their flat or getting funding for their own property. I took the second option because Mum, who is a notorious hoarder, sorry, a social collector, would welcome the extra space—and me too! So, with as much authority as I could muster, I rang the council and told them I had been advised I was eligible for funding for a council house and had been directed to this number. Hey listen, a girl's gotta do what a girl's gotta do—and yes, it worked!

Journey Pause: *There's a saying that you have to "fake it to make it"; and that was certainly true in this case. Dear reader, sometimes in life you have to dress like it, walk and talk like it before you are actually "it"! Don't get me wrong; I'm not advocating a crash-course in how to con people, but it's a proactive method of spring boarding you into where you want to be. Just as putting on a business suit can make you "feel" like you're ready to take on the corporate world (well, it works for me!), so can adopting an assertive, proactive stance help you to actually become what it is that you are portraying. Just thought you'd like to know . . . !*

After numerous application forms later and constantly having to chase Mum to sign here, there and don't forget over the page, we were finally granted the necessary funding to go and find our dream home! Thank you Lord, woooo! However please bear in mind that the rent Mum had paid over the decades could have made her a property magnate if she had invested it in the housing market earlier, but ho hum, never mind, better late than never. So it was official—the house hunting season had begun and I was ready to enter the housing market jungle, armed with determination, a fistful of dollars and a picture of my "dream" house; pleeease, now how HARD could it be?

Journey Pause: *But how many of you know it is not really that easy, especially if you are the one looking on behalf of two people with different tastes and expectations . . . and if it seems the other person is not working with you, trust me, there's going to be trouble in paradise!*

So I off set, armed with my very own house-buying guide for idiots (basically information I'd gotten from the source of all knowledge—the internet!) and began to pound the streets of my local area with a much vigour as my high-heels would allow. Estate agents in the area probably began to groan when I walked in, because in trying to come across as knowledgeable and ultra-confident, questions and comments like: "Does this house have floors and windows? "Oh look! It has walls, ummm, that's good; I'd like more information please!" just gave the game away though, just a little. Okay, maybe I wasn't really that bad but it sure felt it like on reflection! Every week, the collection of potential houses from the local papers just kept on growing, as the newest wannabe homeowner would peruse them for suitable accommodation to meet my decorative style, panache and inherent elegance.

Oh, it was a great time, honestly, because I got the chance to just think outside the box (aka the flat!) and imagine what my dream house could like. However, I have to admit ulterior motives were afoot even when house-hunting as there was guy I liked at the time (he'd been christened "Polyphemus" by my little sister.) I have to confess my house hunting was based in and around the area where he lived. (Seems I was about to become a professional stalker and just move next door! It is just as well I wasn't successful as he moved and relocated not long afterwards . . . to get married . . . ! Hahaha! Oh well!)

During what was to become a rather traumatic phase of my journey, my Mum was her ever phlegmatic self; nothing seemed to move or sway her. To prove my point, she slept through the big storm of 1987. Uh, huh, that's right; when trees were being uprooted and flicked through the air like cocktail sticks, when the wind was on a personal vendetta against bricks and mortar of all shapes and descriptions, when the rain sent drops like bullets against the glass, my Mum, who takes God at His word, was literally asleep in "peace and safety". So with that background and persona, Mum only asked for a garden and a through lounge; apart from that, she was content.

Now me—I wanted it all: front, back, up and down. I wanted a cellar and an attic; I wanted landscaped gardens, a conservatory, an atrium; I wanted an elegant hallway, with French windows in the receptions rooms; I wanted an office-cum-study; I wanted gas central heating AND double-glazed windows. I even wanted nice neighbours, but hey, even I realised there are some things estate agents can not guarantee. Some of the properties we reviewed were amazing, some had bathrooms you could only enter limb by limb—a bit problematic if you ever wanted to use the facilities; painful! I saw a box room for the first time in my life (I tell you, I had a very sheltered upbringing!). It was a tiny, tiny room jammed between two other rooms where you had to go outside just to think and turn around. I saw kitchens that were so tiny, to cook two cans of baked beans would be considered a mammoth task . . . and on and on and on.

But one day, all the house-hunting and property perusing finally paid off and October 1994 was "M-day". We were finally moving to the newly acquired official "Shalisa Residence", a stately 3-bedroom property on the edges of the prestigious "Commonwealth area" in a "well-sought after area in North East London". Okay, okay; it was a cold, mouse infested and damp house, which boasted (!) an all-blue interior décor; I mean ALL-blue ceilings, walls, and skirting boards—in EVERY room! But I loved it, because I could see through the damp and dank to its potential and what it could (and invariably would) be. I really think Mum was probably shell shocked by the whole episode, which might explain her nonchalant behaviour during what was, in hindsight, a really, really exciting time.

Prior to the move, I had arranged everything. (By the way, my personality type is melancholic choleric; I like to plan and organise and boss others while doing it; well, it works for me!) I raided local shopping stores for huge cardboard boxes, where, with a faraway glint in my eyes, I'd imagine myself to be on a house-decorating programme, you know the sort: where you pack in one shot and in the next shot, the proud homeowner is putting up the last of their porcelain figurines on their newly installed Edwardian fireplace . . . sigh. Ha, the reality was that I ended up having to pack up the whole flat, yes I said the whole flat, as Mum had been consigned to simply organising her things (I think I've mentioned my personality type, so you get the picture, okay?). Now, what could possibly go wrong? I thought I could at least concede that to her because if it were left to me, most things would be relegated to the bin. It was a simple and fool-proof plan, or so I thought.

And so the moment finally arrived, the day before the move; it was exciting! I felt my life was now on the up and I was indeed moving ahead; I mean, relocation is an indication of positive growth, isn't it? I had already packed the majority of my worldly goods and knew we had only a few bits and pieces to wrap up; I could barely contain myself! So, with the removal men due to arrive in less than 24 hours, I came home from some last minute shopping, pushed my key in the door for the penultimate time . . . only to find Mum in the kitchen, holding some *old* cake figurines in one hand with a tea towel in the other and a faraway look in her eyes. I could hear read her thoughts as she sat there reminiscing: "Yes, yes, um hum, this one is from back home, yes, the time when Taunty made a nice sponge cake for me. Eh, eh, I wonder what happened to the lady next door's daughter's son's baby. He must be get big by now . . ." Now, I know Mum always likes to take a meander down memory lane but NO, not today! Not now! Not with removal men and a major life changing shift about to take place not to mention the fact we had only hours to completely clean up the flat before returning the key to the council—but not now, not today . . . !

As I took in the scene, my usual loving greeting froze on my lips, and just as well because, what I wanted to say was *not* good. I just glared at her and the scene in the kitchen and then slowly walked towards Mum's room with a growing feeling of foreboding and a sense of no, please let me be wrong. Sad to say, I was not disappointed, as every thing looked as if she was planning on staying for another night or two. Nothing, I mean *nothing* had been packed, opened, undone—nothing, nothing, NOT A THING! The bed was still made up, her clothes were still in the wardrobe, and the chests of drawers were still full . . . Even the curlers and obligatory headscarf were neatly arrayed on the bed (okay, that's a slight exaggeration but still close to the truth!) Needless to say, I was not pleased, not pleased at all; in fact, whatever curly hair I had just straightened and what was straight just knotted and curled up tight, real tight. (With hindsight, I really believe that was the start and the cause of my high blood pressure!) I didn't know whether to pinch myself—or Mum! Let me help you: if you've ever had a dream just shatter at the opening of a door, or even seen a fruit that you really liked and was looking forward to eating only to find it was not as sweet or tasty as it looked, or even a dress that you've been saving to wear for a special occasion only to find it'd shrunk in the wardrobe (yes, that happens to me too!) then welcome to what I was experiencing at that time.

Standing there with the unbelievable now a reality before me, I had to make some swift decisions—NOW! With only hours before the council collected their keys and to ensure Mum and I did not end up sleeping at a bus-stop with all our worldly goods, I took an "executive decision" to cancel the removal men because I knew things were not going to happen as planned (or desired)—and it turned out that I did the right thing. It's at times like these, that one's little "black book" comes in handy and I rang an old flame to see if he was available to help us out of our predicament.

Now Mr. T wasn't so much of an old flame as a glowing ember at the time and boy, he jumped, leaping and whooping, at the chance to give me a "helping hand". To me, he was the original Black "White Van" Man and with his familiar style and swagger, he was my knight in shining armour (well, jeans and t-shirt, but I'm sure you get the picture!) Maybe he thought my calling was to rekindle something between us, to see if we could get moving . . . and sure enough, we got right back into the groove. Between the two of us, we managed to move all of the following—and more—down three flights of stairs: fridges (yes, plural!), the cooker, washing machine, beds, sewing machine, wardrobes, tables, chairs, settees, cuddly toys—and Mum's trunk.

Now, I have to stop here at this moment in my journey, to tell you about Mum's trunk. It really should have had its own show, but it is now a pleasant and thankfully, distant memory (yes!). The "trunk" was a well travelled item, acting more like Mum's travel companion rather than a storage centre or a precursor to today's shopping malls. When opened, it exuded an air of sartorial elegance as the smell of moth balls and mystery would envelope you.

As a child, I loved it when Mum would send me to get the key and with excitement and mystery in the air she would take the key and slowly, seriously and mysteriously unlock the treasure chest. As she'd lift the lid, the magic just grew as treasures from a time long ago would once more be revealed. There was cloth from back home; reams and reams of material, some so old that the fold lines had now become part of the pattern; an assortment of beautiful real lace gloves, so delicate and dainty, a gorgeous black shiny bag, gold bangles and a coin collection from an era where pounds, shillings and pence were the norm. There were real-lace couture dresses for a much slimmer waist (sad to say, including mine): I'm talking Ava Gardner and Audrey Hepburn-type dresses as well as the inevitable figurines and towels, which seem to be as much a part of West Indian culture as mangoes and sunshine.

In hindsight, I now recognise the trunk was a poignant reminder of all that Mum had once been and had left behind. It was her one tangible link to a past where people lived as a family, where children could get a "dust of flour", a touch of salt and a few drops of oil and make fried bakes (a fried savoury dumpling), until dinner time. Each item had its own history, its own tale to tell. Sometimes the "trunk" would be opened and closed quickly as if it didn't want to be bothered but, oh, there were times when it would allow you to read it by touching each treasured item. Those time of reminisce for Mum and a teaching for me about a history and a heritage that seemed a million miles and worlds apart from the council estate of North East London. I just had to acknowledge and salute the role and effect of the "Trunk", which was truly a journey memento if ever there was one!

October 1994 was a date to remember! We did it, we were finally in our new home after much-to-do and in spite of several trips to and from the past to the future and then back again to retrieve items from the communal bin area. Okay, time for me to "fess up and come clean. When I realised Mum was not packed and in no way ready to move, I opted for the move-quick version—just grab and chuck, which is how, let's just say, a few "choice" items ended up in the communal rubbish bin and hence the need for me to keep going back to retrieve items which I guess could be deemed useful: Mum's handbag, her purse and her hot combs—amongst many other precious mementos. (Mum's response when she realised her bag was not where it should be, by her side, was something else, but it sure feels good to get that off my chest at last, phew!)

I had a niggling feeling that maybe, just maybe, our new acquisition might be too small for the contents of a 2-bed flat AND back home memories. I recall all our meagre possessions which had looked so fine and dandy in our previous home (okay, that's probably pushing it a bit!), now looking rather small and tatty. They were ignobly heaped in the corner of the living room, looking like a bunch of awkward guests at an elegant soiree—basically out of place, but so what, we had done it; we were finally in!

Our first Christmas in our new home was exciting; cold but exciting because it was ours. Sadly however, the honeymoon did not last long. After a get-to-know-you period of intense cleaning and polishing, we started to settle in and it was only a matter of time till the cold, cold, reality would kick in, which it literally did in February 1995, when the boiler started to cough and splutter and the antiquated central heating wheezed its way to standstill. Talk about a wake up call. I began to question if I'd done the right thing in taking Mum out of her comfort zone to what was now a cold, damp, dark, dank and draughty house. Life whipped off my rose-coloured glasses and I had an unforgettable "uh-oh" moment. Mice. We had mice. Not cute, Mickey-Mouse-and-friends-type mice but the dark-haired, swift-as-the-wind-type mice. I'd be in the living room and suddenly see a blur of movement out of the corner of my eye and the horrible feeling that . . . "I was not alone" . . . (gulp) and then I'd wonder if I'd really seen something or was it my imagination. Sadly, their dark tell-tale trademarks was proof enough; the truth was indeed out there and living in our house.

I recall one time when I was "fortunate"(?) to preview an exclusive dancing mouse show (for the anti-rodent reader, please feel free to turnover at this point . . .). One day, I was in the kitchen when I suddenly saw a swift movement, but by then, with reflexes having been keenly honed to have made any martial expert proud, I froze and followed the movement to see what and where it. Stealthily and with stalking skills to rival next door's cat, I reached for the long-handled dustpan and brush set (you'll soon see why) . . . and waited silently, deadly and poised. It wasn't long before he the roaming rodent walked into the trap. When the mouse decided it was safe to come back out of its hiding place, he literally to swagger across the floor—and it is then I caught the little so-and-so with the long-handled broom set (ahha, now you know understand why I had it because trust me, I was not about to go eye-to-eye with a mouse . . .). With a ninja move that Jackie Chan would have been proud off, I got him with the broom. However, thought I had at least stunned him with the broom and having, somehow managed to manoeuvre him into the dustpan, I unwittingly relaxed my guard as I was getting ready to throw him into the back garden (look, I'm squeamish about killing them outright, okay) when the mouse revived and probably remembered his training at mouse-survival skills class. I nearly passed out when he moved, but I was not about to be beaten by a rodent, a mouse and my own heightened responses and skills kicked in. It seemed that every bounce he made, I mirrored with the dustpan and broom. Looking back, it was probably the first ever human and mouse dance; maybe he had been taught in mouse school that humans—especially the female of the species—do not like mice, especially when in bouncing mode. It looked like this one had taken lessons from Michael Jackson; not so much "Ben" but a mouse-version of "Thriller" and trust me, it was starting to get really scary, because he didn't run but just kept jumping up at me! Thankfully, my innate sense of resolve and self-preservation prevailed (listen! I was not about to be upstaged and "bounced" by a jumpy mouse) and I finally caught the critter and gladly escorted him to the great outdoors, where hopefully, the neighbour-hood cats have since care of him, thank you very much.

Then there was the cold. The winter of 1994/95 was one of the coldest I can remember. The front door was held up by a nail and a prayer, for the wind always seemed to make itself a welcome guest in our house. If the postman had ever pushed the letters just a little bit harder, I'm sure the door would have given up and given in—literally. The back door was not much better either, as it too was secured by rusty nails, dry rot and a lot of faith. What I had thought was character was now revealed in the cold light of day as rotten. Now that's a lesson right there . . .

Journey pause: *Yes, I'm sure you guessed that one had to be coming at this point! Often what we think is so great, wonderful and exceptional when we're in a state of arousal, which can be based on anything such as embarking on a new relationship to the moment when deciding to get a new pair of shoes, is usually often revealed in it's true colours when our heightened state has past. Just between me and you, it's happened to you too, hasn't it? That hunk turned out to be some chump; that new friend turned out to be Cruella's little sista; that great bargain was the proverbial white elephant. So why is it that we can't see these things in time? What is it or why is it that we tend to blind ourselves from seeing* *things as they really are? Maybe it's a testimony to the fact that humans are, at heart, die-hard romantics and fantasists, always looking for the proverbial pot of gold at the rainbow's end . . . . Oh well, it's all part of our journey, I guess!*

I could go on to tell you of the angst I felt at the time and how stressed out the move made me; I could tell you about the times I would just cry out in bitterness of heart and spirit as I wondered why my dreams never seemed to come true; why, when I would take a step forward I seemed to drop back two? I could tell you how I felt resentful towards the very one I purported to be helping and doing all of this for . . . but I won't. I choose not too. Why, because one of life's great teachers, Time, has taught me to sit and wait just a little bit longer. Remember my vision, my dream for Mum to be settled and to see her put her feet up at the end of a long day? It took a long, long, LONG time . . . but thankfully, the day came when I saw it come to pass. She came in one day, sat down in "her" armchair, reclined and just gave a deep sigh of contentment . . . and my heart felt good, real good . . . and I knew it had been and was indeed, worth it all.

So, what did or have I learned from "The Move": What lessons did I glean for my journey ahead?

1) When life gets ready to move you, don't fight it; just go with the flow.

2) When you choose to move on, to move up and step out, remember your desire for change will attract opposing forces, within and without.

3) Whilst it may look good on paper and on the projector screen of your mind, the reality of doing it and working to bring your vision, your goals and dreams to pass calls for hard work, perseverance, tenacity and a double dose of humour!

4) You learn to laugh at the impossible, as you dare to dream the unthinkable.

You see, although "The Move" was over within a few weeks—I am still living it. Every day, I recognise there are opportunities for me to move from a negative or untruthful way of thinking, living, doing and being—and I have to decide if and how I will choose to do so. So I encourage you to get ready, to start packing up your stuff, cos your journey might be about to move you from one level to another, from existing to living; from trying to doing . . . to **being**. It's a great opportunity and one that you should welcome and grasp with both hands however, as I share *my* journey experience with you just remember—you have been warned, but it will be worth it in the long run . . . so Carpe Diem!

CHAPTER 7

Shhh, Don't Tell!

Sometimes you've just gotta let it out! I mean, how long can you pretend? How long can you keep on trying to "keep on", when what you consider to be the "real you" is literally screaming to come out! So why don't you just go and give in? Because when you recognize there is a call on your life, your life can never really be the same.

*This is all about **our** secrets, yours and mine; those long ago events, shady happenings and fleeting blissful moments. Why secrets? Because there are some things we like to hide—that we need to hide; things, issues, events and memories which need to remain under cover, and the best part is that everyone has secrets! Everyone, all of us, for no one is exempt, loves to hear and tell secrets—just as long as they are someone else's.*

Along my journey, my heart has heard and registered the almost silent sighs and cries, the groans and moans from fellow travellers . . . and on turning aside to listen, I often hear "shhh . . . don't tell" and it is then you begin to get a glimpse of what is truly inside and to get a sense of the depths of the person next to you. Whilst not wanting nor willing to break a confidence, I recognise that in hearing these secrets, my journey has expanded and my life experiences increased vicariously, as I have drawn wisdom from those who have walked a different yet similar path and have been warmed, encouraged and duly inspired.

So, dim the lights, close the curtains, take the phone off the hook and hang a "do not disturb" sign outside the door of your hear because shush, there is something I want to tell you and it could be something you may well need to hear. Some of the following extracts are mine, some are not. In fact, you may even see yourself in one or many of them but know this: these experiences have helped me to walk a little stronger and straighter and in the sharing and telling of them, remember this—you are NOT alone.

No 1: Shhh, Don't Tell . . . .

"My father abused me for years. No, I'm not talking about the hormonal angst teenagers have with Dad dares says "No!" but the abnormal, immoral abuse of the sexual kind. Night sleep disturbed by the family protector and day times haunted by the lingering memories. Knowing he was always watching and wanting me—even when I wasn't there, for isn't the abused always in the eye of the abuser? Knowing innocent laughter would soon turn into unnatural grunts and groans that'd fill the silence of heart. Knowing innocent hugs and kisses would erupt into nocturnal searching, probing and penetration.

Even after Mum died, he probably felt he had a legitimate excuse to turn to me for comfort and "love". I remember on one occasion, laughing along with my other siblings when we discovered condoms in our parent's bedroom, but only I knew on whom and why they were really for. Today's advice to "wrap it up" and "keep it covered" always make me want to throw up. I didn't ask for "it" to be wrapped up or kept covered, hell no! I was—and still am—a child, and I deserved, no, I was the one who needed to be covered and protected. People around me could not understand my antagonism towards men nor my desire to fight, to hit, punch, kick and bite the guys we hung out with. Although always under the guise of "fun", I guess they just assumed I was a militant strong woman. Ha, little did they know, I mean how could they?

How can I now tell my partner my unresponsiveness to his touch in our times of intimacy has its roots in my father's arms? Where do I even begin to tell him that the person he affectionately calls "my old man" is the reason for so much heartache and dysfunction . . . but, please . . . you won't tell . . . will you?"

No 2: Shhh, Don't Tell . . . .

"I was sexually abused by my "aunt's" daughter when was I placed in a pseudo foster system for my care and protection—how ironic. The sick sexual games involved having to perform oral sex on her and even now the vile, disgusting taste of another girl still lingers in my mind. I was not even a teenager at the time and yet abuse, in so many strange and deviant forms, was becoming the norm in my life. Years later, a brother in the family took up the reins. Play fights would quickly evolve into being held down and manhandled as he'd grab, grope and bruise just-formed breasts and try to kiss pre-teen lips. Up to this day, I believe his siblings know, for they'd leave me "wrestling" with him outside their bedroom doors for what seemed like hours until his teenage lust was satisfied and I'd be allowed to crawl downstairs to silently cry inside.

The crunch came when I was 15 years old and alone in their house. When he came home, I was snoozing on the sofa. It's funny, but I can even remember the "high fashion" outfit I was wearing at the time—a long, denim skirt and a burgundy sweatshirt. He came over to where I was on the sofa and I could sense his presence, practically smell his intentions. I thought maybe if I played "dead", he would leave me—but no such luck. I recall (and still recoil from) the memory of teenage hands, themselves yet unformed and unused, now trying to do what more experienced hands would hesitate to do.

I remember a slimy, salivary tongue forcing its way into my mouth when I tried to scream but it was his words "shut up, shut up . . . you know you want it, you know you want it" which still echoes from the distant past to disrupt my present. Shit! Fast moving hands and fingers now forcing themselves between virginal lips and . . . pain. The sharp zing of a zip; his or mine? No, my skirt had buttons down the front, brass-like buttons . . . So no, I know it wasn't my zip—it was his and . . . the feel of an enlarged penis trying to penetrate through nylon panties. Did he rape me? Well, no, he didn't, so I guess I really don't have anything to complain about, do I . . . or do I? It's funny, but even now, I still keep hearing his voice in unwanted, intimate encounters and I freeze, unable to say no, unable to run, unable to plead and beg not to be touched . . . .

. But why dwell on the past; it was a long, long time ago . . . but please, please promise—you won't tell anyone, okay?"

No 3: Shhh, Don't Tell . . . .

"I am on my third abortion. I already have two young children by different men, but have been able to cover it up by pretending they're both for the same man—phew! Don't get me wrong; I have been trying, really trying to get myself together. I got a new job and was able to decorate my flat and even managed to get a new car. Yes, life was looking up and I was doing better. Until the pregnancy test proved otherwise—damn it! This s— was not supposed to happen to me, not now! I was seeing a guy who I thought was "different"—why, I don't know because like attracts like—but he not only broke my heart and took me for a ride, he took my money and my passport as well!

Ha, just when you think you have seen, heard and experienced it all, life reminds you that you ain't seen nothing yet! You see, the baby wasn't his child, oh no, that'd be far too easy, too simple! No, it was his brother's! You see, when he heard what his brother had done and how he had conned me, he came round to offer comfort and support and well . . . we both ended up comforting each other, with inevitable results. I couldn't help myself; I was lonely and hurt and I took whatever comfort I could find—wherever it came from, so don't even bother to judge me, okay!

It was a cold, blustery day when I went to the clinic with my friend, a work colleague who befriended me . . . and who I later betrayed . . . sorry. (Look, I told you s— happens. At this time, even though she was there for me, it's true what they say, isn't it that hurting people hurt. Well, there's no point beating about the bush . . . I took her man, plain and simple, but look, this ain't even about that, okay?) On the day I had a cheerful countenance because I really could not let the mask slip and admit the procedure was becoming a too-familiar routine by now: the hospital bed, the gown, the nurses' professional indifference although to tell the truth, I really did not want to be noticed either. I remember the painful routine—the anaesthetic, the injection and a short, blissful sleep before I woke up—minus myself.

Look, I'm tough, okay; it wasn't even a real baby, so I guess I'll get over it. I've had it before and let's face it, it wasn't the right time nor the right person. I have plans, it's my time! I have so much I want to do and accomplish, don't I? No, it's for the best; it really was the best—and only—thing I could have done. Cry? Me? No, it's just . . . it's just—look, don't worry if you see a couple of tears fall, I guess it's a normal reaction but, hey, please, don't judge me . . . Life happens, but before you go, let's just leave it here and please . . . . . . don't tell anyone else, okay?"

No 4: Shhh, Don't Tell . . . .

"I used to have an affair with a married man. He was much, much older than me and I guess I saw his attention as a form of compensation for the lack of my Dad's inattention and dismissive attitude towards me. You see, my Dad only noticed me long enough to laugh at , ridicule me and lock me out of the house. I did everything I could to get his attention, his approval, his love. Never considered the pretty one, I compensated by excelling academically but all A's, diplomas, being Head Girl and numerous certificates were never enough.

So, when Mr. Married Man began to notice me and look at me and smile at me and laugh with me (instead of at me) and hold me, oh so gently, how could I resist? Many times when he'd take me and my friends' home, mine was the last stop . . . and the first where I'd begin to get to know him in a more intimate way. His closeness, his humour and his intellect stimulated my mind and body. You know, he once gave me some jewellery and I had to pass it off as something from an old friend when friends asked me where it came from—in his presence; I'm sure it's still around here, somewhere . . . I'll try and find it for you another time. Yes, this is one more secret I have to hide but please, this is just between me and you, okay?

No 5: Shhh, Don't Tell . . . .

"I really do not understand this; I mean I am not much to look at! Okay, I'm no stunner or an oil painting, more of a cartoon drawing, really! So how come when I look in the mirror I see someone who is seeing two men at the same time! Two men??!! Believe me when I say that it was not really planned. My first, or should I say, the original one, had gone back home for a long holiday. We had been dating for some months but I could not take the pressure and comments from well-meaning people who kept saying "So kids, when you are getting married then?" "When are you both gonna fix a date" "Oh, I just love to see young love in action!" My blood used to BOIL! So when No. 1 went off to visit his family it was a welcome relief—freedom from the comments and, if I'm honest, from him too! It soon evident the latter end was worse than before. Now the "well-meaning" comments changed from "When's the date" to "Where is he?" to "Where's the postcard; you mean, he's been gone so long and no postcard or even a phone call? Why the delay?", and then finally: "So, what you going to do?" Arrgghh! I was tired, fed up and ashamed because their questions only served to remind me that I had been unceremoniously dumped—or so I thought.

It was at a friend's dinner party that I met him or rather, he met me. At the table, I noticed his eyes, his brash, friendly almost arrogant manner and beautiful smile and the accent: an island rawness which really appealed to me. He "noticed" me by commenting on my size whenever I would ask for another helping of food: "What! You want another helping? I wouldn't if I were you" and once again, I reverted back to being the proverbial after-dinner joke. I sat and seethed for the rest of the meal, angry at him, them and myself for being attracted to such a rude, odious man—with lovely eyes. Then the unexpected happened. He needed a lift and would you believe it, my services were volunteered. So I was now promoted from joke material to chauffer, wow! I agreed because to have declined would have attracted more derisory comments from everyone . . . So with head held high and butterflies in my stomach, we walked to my car. All thoughts of "him overseas" were now out of my mind.

I started to drive and we started to talk—properly. It was a friendly banter at first until he asked me directly: "So, when can I see you?" My heart jumped—literally! You know what I mean! I'm talking about the bass drum you hear in your ears and the thump, thump, thump in your chest as you try to focus on getting your breathing right. I almost had a cardiac in the car! I have to confess though, it felt good to know Mr. Man liked me . . . me! However, reality kicked in and with all the dignity I could muster I replied "Sorry, but I'm seeing someone" and I recall feeling such a hypocrite when I said it, because this man, this man right here, right now, sitting in my car was H.O.T!! Everything in me was screaming for him when he unexpectedly replied: "Girl, I didn't ask about him, I asked about you"—and that did it for me! I stuttered and struggled with wanting to be faithful and knowing I should turn him down—and my desire to take it further. Well! I met Mr. Man the next day and we went to London Zoo. I still remember us walking across Tower Bridge hand-in-hand and we ended up at his house for a little anthropology research of our own. There's an old saying that "stolen waters are sweet, and bread eaten in secret is pleasant". Our illicit affair began and continued when my boyfriend (finally) returned. What made matters worse was that we all moved in the same circles, so at social events, I'd sit there with my boyfriend and Mr. Man knowing I had a double portion which I was loathe to give it up and let go . . . . Still, it's all water under the bridge now, isn't it? I mean, no one was hurt, I mean really hurt and I guess, no harm was done, well, not really . . . but hey, you won't tell will you?"

No 6: Shhh, Don't Tell . . . .

Well, I guess compared to others, this is probably the one that got away but it's a little secret I've never really shared . . . until now. Don't laugh, but I had the "hots" for someone young enough to just look over the sweet counter at Woolies (now that's a blast from the past, hahaha!) Let me see . . . I was nearing the big 4.0. and let me tell you, I felt a sense of empowerment like never before; I had arrived—or at least, I was on my way. I knew how to walk, talk, dress and act to get a man (the fact that I was always single and/or in-between relationships is neither here nor there) and the man I wanted was just barely legal . . . but boy, was he ever ready! Don't be fooled and think it's only men who have a hard time holding back in coming forward—women suffer too!

Every time I'd dropped him home, we'd sit and talk; you know those conversations where one word, literally dripping with potential and intent, can change the atmosphere in a moment. Well! This particular night was one that I'll never forget. I contrived to make sure I dropped him off last (I'm the driver, so the car goes where I want, ha-ha!) We parked up outside his house and as he talked to me, I was making love to him in my mind; I mean, hot, sweaty and steamy. Excuse me while I go back in time! I'm talking sauna hot! Arabian Desert and midnight at the oasis hot! We were cooking with gas, baby! He'd smile and in my mind, I was on him, literally! When he talked and moved his hands, I'd picture them coming towards me and . . . well . . . (Phew! Is it getting in here or is it just me?!) The fact we were usually discussing innocuous issue like current affairs and his university choices (!) did not really matter; they were merely the dressing for the main meal set before me—him!

One night, it almost happened: I'd dropped him home and we were seated in my car, talking innocently when suddenly, in the midst of it all, the atmosphere changed. C'mon ladies, you know what I mean! One minute the air is clear and the next, you feel like you've been running through a hot, steamy jungle on an extremely hot day. Pheromones started oozing from all parts of my body—even my eyelids! He stopped and had the cheek to flash a brilliant white, I mean WHITE Colgate "ting" smile at me before he turned to face me, full on, with a look that plainly said he'd read my mind, had been reading it all along and well, it was my move. All it needed was one touch, a slight nod, a faint sigh, a gentle breeze to set it all in motion. There's an old saying about being "weighed in the balances and found wanting". Look, let me just be real; the only thing I was wanting was young man body on mine—no lie.

Time seem to stop and in that moment, I was forced to weigh up the pros and cons of making such a move and the inevitable fall out, because where would such a "relationship" go? What mileage could it ever have? Truth to be told, inside I was saying "Damn the mileage, I just want to start the engine right here, right now!" Sorry, but that's the freak in me and believe me when I tell you, he was ready; I know what I'm talking about. We never touched—physically—but there are times when a touch is something "after the fact", because we'd already connected in our spirit, our minds and in our emotions. I struggled with the fact that I was old enough to be his mother which back then was considered more a taboo than it is nowadays. I reasoned it'd never work but, even as I tell you this and relive the moment, I can still feel the heat of the temptation, lust and desire that was burning me . . .

Well, after what seemed like several lifetimes and some breath-taking moments, I, *we*, came back to our, *my* senses. C'mon, I was a grown-ass woman with responsibilities and what could a just-out-of-college boy have to offer me, anyway? I literally, frantically pulled myself together, stopped hyper-ventilating and said good-bye. Would you believe I was kicking myself when I drove off, as I was now wishing I'd seized the moment—and him—because unless you try, you'll never know, right? Well, that's my little secret of the one who got away but hey, let's just keep it between the two of us, okay? I've got a reputation to keep!

No 7: Shhh, Don't Tell . . . .

The following was given by "Marylyn" who first agreed for it to be shared at a women's conference in 2009. She has always been keen to tell her story and I had to include this one as the final traveller's tale of . . . . *Shhh, Don't Tell . . . . !*

> *"For they overcame by the blood of the Lamb and by telling and sharing the power of their testimony" Revelation 12:11*

I was privileged and honoured to spend over a week in the company of an extraordinary woman. God had engineered our meeting and I believe it was an opportunity to share one woman's story, the "power of her testimony" at the Conference, "From Gutter to Glory". Please listen as I share Marylyn's story . . . .

Whilst elements of my story may not be unique, it's in piecing them together, like a family quilt, that I can see the wonderful hand of God and I can now see that there's a purpose for my life.

"You little red wretch you! You was trouble from the day you was born! Yes you, you little dry stick, you! I was 28 days in the hospital because you wouldn't come out! Nothing but trouble, nothing but trouble, nothing but trouble"

That was my inauguration into this world almost 60 years ago; that was my welcome speech, my arrival song. The 2nd of 11 children, I began to know the meaning of abuse from an early age; in fact, it became a way of life . . . my life.

I was taken out of school before my 11th birthday to help my mother look after other people's children—a baby taking care of other babies! When they wanted feeding, it was me; when they wanted dressing, it was me; and guess who had to change nappies? That's right—me! My younger siblings tapped into the fact that I was the family whipping post and readily supplied the stories and tales that would ensure yet another beating, another shouting—another portion of abuse. I don't know what it was, but my mother seemed to take delight in lashing out at me; why, I will never know.

My father left home when I was 6 years old, to go to England. It was years, years later that I found out that he used to send money for us via his sisters, my aunts—but because they didn't like my mum, we never got the money! I discovered this one day when, as a young woman, I confronted him about it. I was angry and hurt and wanted to know how and why he just left us fatherless and penniless. Have you ever seen a grown man cry? As the tears fell silently down his face, I began to realise that maybe, he too, was also a victim; seems I was right, as the money he had sent, never reached us.

At the age of 13, after yet another beating, I remember a specific prayer that I made; even though I didn't know much about God, I remember just speaking to Him. "God, where are You? Do you know me? Do you exist? Well, if you do and you can hear me, please listen. I want two children; the girl first and then the boy. I want to make someone to love and to love me back." I always tell people to be careful what you ask for! At the age of 15, my "prayer" was answered, and the second miracle came 2 years later. So I became a mother of two at the tender age of 17- and that's when the trouble started.

Being a child is one thing, but having children while still a child is another. I remember the words, the scorn, and the spite that was thrown on me. I remember having to sleep in a tiny, tiny bed (though I was grateful for the bed). Only my son was allowed to sleep with me as my daughter had to sleep on a blanket bed on the floor. I used to wait until people were sleeping then put her in the bed with me. At nights, when the man of the house would pass by to empty the chamber pot (in those days!), I would have to use my body as a shield to cover my children from the urine that would splash over onto them. I would have to spend nights sitting in the town square after dark, with the baby in my arms and my daughter sleeping next to me, because I could only get into the house after dark.

One night, I had had enough. Enough of the pain, the words, the suffering, especially seeing my children suffer—and I decided to take matters into my own hands. I went to the doctor and lied and told him that I was having trouble sleeping and he gave me what I thought was my way out—sleeping pills.

I went home that day, with the intention to give my children first and then myself, because I know no one would look after them if I just took myself alone. But God! There was an old lady also sharing the house a "mother", who we all called "dada". She was a woman who had dedicated her life to God and was always praying. She usually went to church but that particular evening she came home earlier than usual. Around 8.30pm that evening, when she should have been out, and I was getting ready to kill me and my children, she was home. She looked at me and said "Marylyn, come here. I want to have a word with you." I went, not knowing or expecting what was to come. "Marylyn, where's the bottle? Give me the bottle! God showed me what you plan to do, so just give me the bottle". I froze! No one else, NO ONE else knew—but God. "You can't give life, so why take it?" And right there and then, Dada taught me to pray. "Marylyn, just talk to God like you're talking to me".

That is what I did and we've been talking ever since I was 19 years old. I try my best to be sincere with Him—and myself too. Just walk with Him and let His love lead, cover and fill you.

Marylyn has endorsed this written testimony

Conclusion . . .

Shhh, don't tell—but sometimes you've just gotta let it out! I mean, how long can you pretend? How long can you keep on trying to "keep on", when what you consider to be the "real you" is literally screaming to come out! So why don't you just give in? Stop the struggling, the internal fighting and distress because when you recognize there is a call, that there's a purpose and destiny for you to be here, yes, even reading this book, your begin to realize your life can never really be the same. This chapter is to help you realise you are not on your own. You've gone through some bad things but there are others worse off than you. Even if your story is worse, it doesn't matter; you've made it through, you're here still standing; you're a survivor!

A friend told me the other day that God says "it doesn't matter where the mess came from or how it got there, I Am able to clear it up! Just give it to me; I'll take care of it". When I heard that, it was like water to a thirsty man. You see, we can cover up and think it's all gone, but unless we deal with our own past hurts and are honest enough to come forward, the past will continue to be our future, irrespective of how we try to mask it with the latest make up, fashion and designer clothes.

Sometimes on our journey, our secrets become hidden, destroying weights and unseen but formidable hurdles which hinder us from moving on and going forward.

Sistas, it's time to open up . . . be honest first and foremost with yourself. Allow yourself time to go back and heal, to go back and review . . . to go back and forgive yourself. Allow yourself time to wrap your arms around the person you used to be and release the comfort and love you've been looking for. Go on, you can do it; it's time to take off those old and worn bandages you've been using to cover up your festering wounds. It's time to let light and air get to it so the healing process can begin. Because that is what you're in need of—healing. Only you know where to apply it, because you know you. It's time to look in the mirror and see yourself: broken but still standing; wounded but still alive; hurting but still able to love, in spite of all what life has done to and even through you.

Use the pain of your past to propel you forward into your purpose and destiny; let life's obstacles become your opportunities; let life's stumbling blocks become your stepping stones; let life's hurdles become your means to come up higher!

Shhh, don't tell? Sista, it's time to take back your power, so open your heart, straighten your shoulders, look yourself and life squarely in the eye . . . and sista, it's time to walk and talk!

No. 8 Shh, Don't Tell: One Mo' Story!

Now, just when I thought I'd finished this chapter "Shhh . . . Don't Tell!" there was a sense of unfinished business still within me. I tried to ignore it but it just wouldn't leave me alone, rather like an inner urge for double-chocolate fudge cake (okay, okay, that's my *dream!) So at the gentle insistence of the memory of Ms X, which kept asking to be included in this particular episode, I am compelled to share the following aspects of this person's life journey.*

(Please note: I managed to track down and tell Ms X what I was being gently nudged to do, because I recognise that in the telling, there is healing and in the hearing, there is deliverance.)

In preparing this additional excerpt, an old church chorus came to mind. It is not an obvious one as is does not feature in the latest gospel hip-hop & R&B chart, but the words sum up the essence of Ms X—past, present and future:

> *"I will serve Thee because I love thee, You have given life to me;*
> *I was nothing before You found me, You have given life to me.*
> *Heartaches, broken pieces, Ruined lives are why you died on Calvary*
> *Your touch was what I longed for, You have given life to me . . ."[1]*

It could be me, it could be you—it could be a reflection of where we have been or a dire warning of what could be ahead. So, welcome to Ms X's story, a piece of real "her-story", the final instalment in this section and as you read, be warned and remember . . . "Shhh, Don't Tell!" Over to you, Ms X . . .

---

[1]   © Copyright 1969 by William J. Gaither. International copyright secured. All rights reserved. Used by permission.

Ms X's Story . . .

"Okay, okay now I've given my approval for this to be included but wow, it is still very painful. It is like recovering from a major operation; you know you've now been healed and put back together but you're still vulnerable and woozy from the anaesthetic. So please bear with me if I seem to skim over some issues or just plain leave them out, because even being able to remember and allow myself to recap is a miracle in itself.

Now, how can I described myself: I love to look good; not overtly glamorous (I leave that to Shalisa, smile!) and have been described as being elegant and classic. Yes, I guess that would sum me up—and yes, I am going to admit it is a façade, a cover that has helped to carry me over and through many a stormy mile in my life and believe me, I've seen a few!

There are too many stories and incidents; for in some ways, my journey experiences parallels those already shared; the pain of having loved too much, too long and too hard, yes, I've been there too. However, there was one major incident that I now feel strong enough to share. Forgive me if I stumble in the telling because it is still sore and painful but I think I'm now healed enough to be able to touch and talk about it—just, only just . . .

Hmmm, where to start? Now, I'd gotten out of a dysfunctional marriage that had flat lined a long, long time before, by meeting the ultimate love of my life. I was young—and so was he—and when I met him on a beautiful sun-kissed paradise beach, I didn't know whether it was the sand, sea or sun that relaxed me enough to lower my guard but I just threw caution—and my marriage—to the wind. After a physically intense and emotionally charged relationship aka courtship that included separation, divorce and a baby, my love and new husband were finally able to be together. My life was now complete. After all the years of pervious heartache and broken promises, I finally had someone who truly loved me.

Then one day—*it* happened. You know, we women always swear that we would never let a man do this or that to us because we wouldn't turn "ninja" on them, but that is always until the first time *it* happens. The first time is always the start, never the end. Sistas—please take it from me—the raised eyebrow can suddenly become the raised voice and then the raised fist. My "ever loving husband" slapped me—ME—and I froze, still, ice-cold still as the heat of the moment burned itself on my memory. The realisation of what had just happened seemed to hold me in an icy embrace. All my bold talk, my chat, my self-esteem was suddenly stripped away and the one who should have been my covering and protector was the one responsible. I went from having a loving husband to a live-in abuser.

However, did I tell? Hell no! That was not me at all! Isn't it funny how pride and low self-esteem can co-exist in the same place at the same time? My pride would not and couldn't let me disclose what was happening to me and I started to disappear before my own eyes. At that time, to look at me, you'd have never guessed anything was going on between us. I was always quick to recognise and deflect any sign of his quick and ignorant temper when we were at social gatherings because he knew I hated public showdowns. Don't get me wrong: I always gave as good as I got, especially if we were in a public place, but I knew there'd be a price to pay on the way home and when we arrived. I made sure I was always poised, polished, seeking to exude a stylish and fashionably classic style on the outside but no amount of designed fragrance could cover the stench of being in an abusive relationship.

Then one day, it all came spilling out, it had too! Let's face it, sistas; there is only so much a dustbin can hold before it starts to smell and fall out, for no matter how much you push it down, when the limit is reached, that's it.

I was at a friend's house. We'd all arranged to go and yes, he had given me permission (!) for me to go but abusers are also manipulators. They will agree to do or give or "allow" something, usually something you've waited, planned and hoped for, but will inevitably manage to manipulate events at the last minute, so they have the sadistic pleasure of watching your reaction as they effectively shatter your dreams. That night was no exception. The constant bickering which had started when we left home had grown into the usual slap and push drama that was becoming like a too-familiar TV sit-com rerun, only without an off button to end it. As I said before, I tried standing up to him but what chance has a kitten against a roaring loin? Yep, that was a wonderful, happy, blissful marriage. Ha!

We arrived at my friend's house where, having learned to cover the tears and hide the pain, I used a retouch of face powder, neutral lipstick and eye shadow to paint on bright eyes and a happy smile, my usual mask. It's funny, but having gone through this experience, I believe I can usually discern those tell-tale signs which are barely visible below picture perfect make up. There is a silence which screams out for help and deliverance; there's the barely noticeable shifting of body weight from one foot to another as if the person, usually a sister, is debating whether to run now or later . . . or at all. It is in the ever-shiny eyes where one tear, having escaped, threatens to unlock those left behind. Its slow path to freedom down the side of her face is a story which her mind is afraid to admit to itself, much less to tell someone else.

My friend greeted us and although I yearned to just run to her and breakdown, I resisted. Even though I knew she had my back, I was not ready to burden her with my issues when she herself was going through her own relationship roller coaster. I guess it was also pride that held me back; pride and a sense of where on earth would I begin? Tell me, how do you confess that you're in such a place, to a person who's always seen and known you as the level-headed one, the rational thinker? Someone who's been able to walk tall, head high and shoulders back through all the stuff life has thrown at me. We sat down and my friend went back upstairs to finish getting ready. My husband and her boyfriend, who knew each other, started chatting about old time but I could feel the tension growing in the room between us, rather like when the air gets "heavy", just before a storm breaks. Then suddenly, somehow, the storm broke; I can't remember from where or when but my husband and I ended up in the hallway, exchanging harsh words, which I knew from past experience would only have one outcome. Maybe it was Dutch courage coupled with the belief and hope that, *surely*, surely, he'd never hit me in public; maybe I thought he'd be breaking an unspoken rule if he did. However, abusers seem to have an inbuilt need to expand their power base. No longer content with bullying, manipulation and manhandling in public, they seem to develop and promote into higher things, as their intimidating behaviour now starts to leak out. (Sistas, as my friend likes to say: "If a man hits you once, it's two times too many!")

As body pushes became tight squeezes and slaps, my friend, who was now downstairs, heard the commotion, suddenly flung open the door and said: "Listen! What's going on here? Not inside of here, please! If you have to kill her, please do it outside; not in here; I'm not used to this kind of thing". Then she promptly shut the door! It's funny how a memory can be etched on forever in your mind and on your psyche. Wow, my friend, my good friend, was willing to leave me in my state, with the caveat that, if I'm to be killed, to at least have the decency to do it outside; trust me, that took a lot of coming to terms with . . .

As I stood there, mulling over this strange yet familiar place that I now seemed to be living in, another friend, LS, arrived. Sensing something was not quite right, she called an emergency meeting in the kitchen. I don't recall saying much as it was my first friend who was talking on my behalf and getting angry about how we were practically going at it, hammer and nail, in her house! It was then I took a deep, deep breath and told them that my husband had slapped me across the face only hours earlier. Now, there are some things you don't tell certain people, especially women and NOT if you happen to be in a kitchen at the time (too many pots, pans and knives). At the telling of what had happened, I felt safe, surrounded by "my girls", strong, no-nonsense women, of whom I was one (or at least used to be), and they were waiting for an excuse to "christen" a newly-bought frying pan on my husband's head (this was my friend's idea but believe me, I was certainly tempted! After hearing this news, my friend who's house we were in just grabbed my hand and marched me upstairs to talk to her.

Now my friend's Mum was, and still is, calm and soothing, unlike my friend who's rather fiery to say the least!

"Tell her, go on Ms X; tell her" and while I struggled to know how to begin, I heard my friend say: "Mum! The little *%!@ * hits her and I'm sure it's not the first time, either!"

At this stage, I think I was beginning to wonder if it wasn't safer outside with my "ever-loving husband" than having to deal with a very irate friend, who was mad, bad and furious—but I knew it was because she was very upset at what had happened.

Being in that room was a haven for me, a time portal, where I could drop the pretence, the façade, and the shame—and just allow myself the freedom for pent up tears to fall. I felt safe in my friend's Mum's bedroom where I free to speak about the abuse without any shame or recriminations. Her Mum's words gently but lovingly rebuked and soothed at the same time:

"Ms X, what happened? How did you get yourself into this? My dear, you are too nice a girl to allow some man like *that* to put his hand on you! Oh gosh man, you are too nice!"—and I cried even harder. For at that time, I remembered my own Mother's domestic situation and it suddenly seemed as if life was on an unwanted repeat cycle, as if I had drawn the proverbial short straw and I was now on a path I'd witnessed but had sworn I've never walk.

BANG, BANG! "Open the door! I want to speak to my wife! (BANG, BANG!) Open the door!".

I nearly jumped out of my skin as the "flight-or-fight" adrenaline kicked in but it was more flight because by then, it felt as if all my fight had long gone. BANG, BANG! Surely he'd never be so bold and so brazen as to just walk in. would he? Oh God, please, please don't let him come in.

(When I'd relieved this time with my friend she said that anyhow, ANYHOW the door had even cracked open, it would have been all over—and knowing my friend can be quite a firecracker when she's ready, I believed her! My friend was ready to fight because there was NO way she'd have allowed a man, and that type of man in particular, to come into her Mum's bedroom.)

I've heard people say that in certain situations, time stands still and I can testify to that. Every character in this domestic drama—my friend, her

Mum and my enraged husband—seemed to be within their own freeze frame.

"Listen, she's inside here, talking to my Mum and will be out in a few minutes".

"I want to speak to my wife—NOW!!"

"LOOK! I said she's inside here talking to my Mother and will be with you in a few minutes". By this time, my friend was icy calm—too calm—and that's not a good sign, believe me.

I vaguely remember hurriedly finishing our conversation; and being held and hugged by Mum. I felt strengthened and empowered. When I left Mum's bedroom, it was with a little hope, a little courage and a little more self-respect. Why? Because I realised someone was still able to love and respect *me* at a time when it being beaten out of me, both verbally and physically. Slowly, oh so very slowly, I was able to open up and reveal, bit by painful bit, the truth about my marriage. It is not easy being so vulnerable and open, even to a life-long friend, and no one, no matter how close you are to them, likes to have to go deep within themselves, much less to share it with someone else.

Well, I'd like to say it ended that night; I'd like to say that was the last of such events but, you've guessed it. It went on behind closed doors, with similar eruptions often occurring at family gatherings as well as in front of the children. In the years that followed, I finally realised what it was that God saved me from, when what my now-estranged husband had meant for me ended up with another sista losing her life at his hand. But that's another story for another time and place.

I just wanted to share this story, I *had* to share this story with you. Why? Because domestic violence is fast becoming the norm; a push, a shove, a slap, verbal put-downs, emotional tug-of-wars all add up to being abused by someone you love because, let's face it, the majority of domestic violence is seldom carried out by a total stranger. No, it's usually someone you love and trust.

So to those reading this—if you have experienced or are experiencing domestic violence in any shape or form:

1) Be honest about the reality of the situation, firstly with yourself. Don't try to cover it up with makeup, comfort eating, retail therapy, or some other emotionally charged negative reactive behaviour.

2) Be honest with others. A family member, a close friend—or even an observant person who may be able to tell you what you're trying to hide from yourself. Honour yourself enough to be still and listen; it could just well save your life;

3) Don't be distracted by broken promises, heartfelt tears or sweet, passionate love-making; trust me, physical abuse is NOT foreplay, so don't get it twisted. No amount of "I'm-so-sorry-and-won't-do-it-again" sex, no matter how sweet, can mend a broken heart or a wounded spirit;

4) Recognise your situation: get help and get out! If you're single, get out. If you've got children, get out. Don't allow anything or anyone to keep you in an abusive relationship. Don't allow the abuser to use them to blackmail you into staying so they can manipulate and control you. One day it is you; the next it could well be them . . .

5) Cry. That's a strange one but there are different types of tears. There are those that reflect pain and sorrow, there are those that release anger and rage, there are those that speak for you when you cannot speak out for yourself—and there are those tears which heal. It is time to let the healing begin.

6) Love again—and start with you. It is time to be still, to reflect and recuperate. It is time to rebuild your self-esteem, self-confidence and your own personal relationship with yourself. Read one or two relevant books to help you begin to know yourself and to get the courage to take the next positive steps.

7) If you can, PRAY! (This advice comes highly recommended). Cry out to God from the depth of your soul. If you can't speak out loud, just "talk" to Him in your mind. Even if you *don't* believe in God, just the action of talking to a Bigger Someone is therapeutic. Still cry out and pray—who knows Who will hear you from across eternity to stretch out a hand to help you.

Oh dear, I think I better stop now; the memories are too much and Shalisa is signalling she wants her pen back, so thanks for listening but please, I ask you as I've asked her . . . shhh, promise you won't tell, okay?"

For anyone experiencing domestic violence in any form, please contact any of the following organizations as a first step to coming out of an abusive relationship:

Helpline	Phone number	Opening hours
National Domestic Violence Helpline	0808 2000 247	24 hours a day
Northern Ireland Domestic Violence Helpline	0800 917 1414	24 hours a day
Scottish Domestic Abuse Helpline	0800 027 1234	24 hours a day
Wales Domestic Abuse Helpline	0808 80 10 800	24 hours a day
Men's Advice Line (for male victims of domestic violence)	0808 801 0327	Monday-Friday, 10am-1pm and 2pm-5pm
Dyn Wales Helpline (for male victims of domestic violence in Wales)	0808 801 0321	Monday and Tuesday, 10am-4pm. Wednesday, 10am-1pm

Southall Black Sisters	020 8571 9595	Monday-Friday, 10am-5pm
(for black women victims of domestic violence)	(calls are not free)	
Domestic Abuse Information	*http://www.hiddenhurt.co.uk*	
Home Office Information	*http://www.ukba.homeoffice.gov. uk/while-in-uk/domesticviolence*	

CHAPTER 8

Sista to Sista

You've probably guessed from my journey journals thus far that I like to dip into my experiences to share a little of life's lessons I have gleaned to date. Now, I dare not say "learned" because life often has a way of reminding me I am still in class and graduation is still a long, long way ahead. But there are times when life will call you up to the front of the class to recite what you have learned thus far . . . and guess what? If you're good, I mean really good, life awards you a gold star!

Well, it's my turn to step up front and "show and tell" the following nuggets with my sistas. Trust me, these have been gained during long, lonely nights of intense study, midnight-candle burning sessions and lots of tears and prayers. Compared to some, my few experiences may seem somewhat paltry but I have learned to thank God for them, because one sista's pain is another sista's precaution. This chapter is the reflection of some of the twinkling stars from my brief experiences, which I hope will help to shed a little extra light on another sista's journey. Sometimes, it's as if I'm hearing myself ask question to which I have painfully gained an answer. Note: not *the* answer but *an* answer, because where and what I have learned has been according to my curriculum, but I am willing to share any of the transferable elements, in the hope someone, maybe *you*, will find them useful . . .

Today, I chatted to a work colleague at work and during the course of the conversation, heard myself ask her if she was seeing or dating anyone at the moment.

Journey Pause: *I'm pausing at this point to explain the difference between "seeing" or "dating" someone, as based on my journey* *experiences, as well as from those gleaned from my interactions and conversations with other fellow travellers:*

> *"Seeing" someone is, I believe a mutual "booty" call. It's an unwritten but mutually accepted agreement that you're both "with" each other in the moment; i.e. it's saying that when you're together, you're together and when you're not, you're not. Seeing does not necessitate any real commitment with the person involved; it just is. "Dating" however involves a (hopefully!) mutual decision to meet someone, usually the person of your affections and desire, in advance and the very nature of the word serves to define the nature of said meeting. In most Western cultures, "dating" is usually with an assumed end in mind for both parties (either sex or marriage, depending on which end of the spectrum you are at!) Sadly, many sistas are "seeing" men all the while believing they're "dating" them and many brothas are afraid to "see" a sista, even on a platonic relationship, just in case she gets the wrong idea and think they're now "dating"! Oh, the complexities of life . . . !*

Now, I really didn't mean to get into the personal side of life with my work colleague, as it really was none of my business as to what, where and with whom she was doing, because I know I wouldn't (and still don't) want anyone to be so inquisitive in my affairs either! However, there are times when an inkling and a prompting will push me to step outside of my comfort zone to end up in a place I had no intention of going. I "heard" myself asking her the question and at first, she hesitated, but it was a hesitation you do when you're deep down, glad to have been asked. It was a hesitation which indicated a longing to respond, when deep down, you're really not sure if you should, could or would even be able to dare to speak it out loud.

After a while, I heard " . . . Yes, but . . . humm"

Now her response spoke volumes! You see, when a woman is safe, secure and loved in a reciprocal relationship, believe me, being in such a relationship, it just flows; there is no stopping her! Because as previously explained, "seeing" someone is very different from being in a relationship and it's a term we tend to apply to someone we're just "knocking boots with" (now *that's* an old-fashioned phrase; it's a bit graphic but true, nonetheless!) As the sista continued to open up, it turned out to be a sad but oft-repeated scenario: Mr Man pursues, Mr Man gets his prey, Mr Man suddenly seems to forget why and what he was chasing in the first place; Ms Sista then takes over where *he* left off and now *she's* chasing, while he's now still and going no where with her and is probably on the lookout for another prey . . .

Given the nature of the conversation, we didn't' want to be overheard by other work colleagues and we thankfully found an empty office. I then said to her: "You know, I don't usually ask people if they are seeing anyone, but I felt prompted to do so. Would you mind if I shared a little something with you, that I've gained from own experience?" (Believe me, there's nothing like a little personal perspective to help the medicine go down!)

"First of all, sista, you have got to know, define and maintain your boundaries. Let me guess: Mr Man was chasing and saying and doing all the right things but did he actually *say* anything to you about wanting to take this relationship further? No? Then this is where you need to listen to what he actually is saying and **not** to what he's doing!"

Journey Pit Stop! *Let me break it down for y'all . . . You see, too often we sistas get excited by what the man-of-the-moment is doing; flowers, candlelight, romantic dinners, back rubs (I'll stop there.!) but in the midst of all this, we have failed to realize the man has not actually committed himself, for he knows that anything he effectively says can and will be used in evidence against him! So that is why a lot of men will give things instead of actually committing themselves by saying "Hey Sista! I like you and would like to make it work/take it to the next level/think you could be the one" (Okay, the last one is my wishful thinking!).*

Whilst this going on, what is Ms Sista doing in the meantime? Why, she's on automatic lockdown; the flowers and chocolate, the wining and dining (even it if it's just a Big Mac by candlelight) all touch a nerve and strike a chord within her. She puts up a "sold subject to contract" sign, when all Mr Man was doing was taking a perfunctory viewing of the property. She stops considering anyone else because, in her mind, she is in an "exclusive relationship"—especially if sex is involved. Ah sex, there it is, folks, that little 3-letter word with a whole lotta of impact! It's an elusive something, which is akin to money. We all want and need a little, but don't really want people to know just how much we're after! We all love it—but just want to make out we're not really interested! We've probably read, heard or even experienced where, in general, women tend to enter sexual relationships as a sign of their "love", whereas men (generally speaking) will say they love a woman in order to get the goods (sex, sex, sex!) So imagine the situation: he's "seeing" her (and sexing her to boot) while she thinks they're in an exclusive-we're-going-somewhere relationship, not knowing that from the man's perspective, they've already reached as far as he's prepared to go! Did he actually tell her the relationship has mileage, potential, that it is truly going somewhere? Hmmm, hope that made some you think for a while!

When I put it to Ms Sista today, she had to agree. I could see the flicker of "oh-my-goodness" start to light up in her eyes, as she realized that, once again, she'd fallen for the "watch-what-I-do-not-what-I-say" tactic. She admitted that yes, in the beginning he was hot and sweaty; his phone calls would have helped BT to easily surpass their profit margin in a very short time, but when he realized the prey had been caught, the chase was off and he cooled off. From my own experience, I refer to this as the "caught-and-cold" period: Mr Man pursues, catches and then cools off. If the relationship has moved quickly and is now based on the physical, then what else is there for him to consider, when he has it all? Now, for any men reading this, please don't feel offended; but let's be honest, it's only you and me here, because as space is seen as the final frontier, so "sex" is seen as the final frontier within the relationship stratosphere.

Know Your Worth!

I reminded Ms Sista to begin to seriously redefine her boundaries; to set parameters and to make a conscientious effort to operate within them. When you *know* your worth and your place in life, when you are confident and comfortable to stay and operate within it, any prospective Mr. Man will learn he had better step up to the plate in order to step in;

because you're not budging! Yes, it's not very politically correct; in fact, it's well nigh old-fashioned but true nonetheless: Mr. Man will only want what he thinks is exclusive. Every time we decide to lower our standards to step out and down, I believe Mr. Man gets a little disappointed. In the meantime, other prospective suitors come by, but because *we* think we're in an exclusive relationship, we send them off, whether consciously or unconsciously, without even hearing what they have to offer.

Honestly, I think sistas need to have a more objective, business-like approach to relationships. Basically, Ms Sista should not put her best cards on the table—until she is sure of her negotiating parameters and position. Thus, if another offer then comes along offering better prospects, she's potentially placed to consider it, without having compromised herself and caused the other person to feel they've been gazumped!

Ms Sista sat and listened to my theorising and personal philosophies. Have you ever watched a sunrise; you know, that magical moment when the sun just peeps over the horizon and lights up your whole view? Well, that's what happened to Ms Sista; she began to realize that where she was, was not representative of who or what she deserved. As women, we have to recognize the part we play, whether knowingly or not, in our own demise. It could be we haven't established our boundaries, that we're trying to fit a societal and cultural mould that is not our size, shape or season; or maybe we're just plain lonely and don't want to be left on the proverbial shelf.

All these and a score of other reasons are what we allow to undermine ourselves and the sad thing is, we end up attracting men who serve to keep us in that negative position. So how can we get out? By seeking to be still and listen to yourself, to your inner you. You truly need to be still so you can hear what your heart is saying to you. Just as you'd have a plan, a checklist when buying a house or a car (and if not, you now know you have to get one!), you need to establish such a plan for your personal-relationship life, because without that kind of life-protection plan, you're setting yourself up for failure. . . .

Now back to Ms Sista! The impromptu "therapy session" came to an end and when I got back to my desk, I found the following email from Ms Sista:

> *"You are an angel! This has been bothering me for a while. There are a few guys interested but been sending them off. Now I know. Once again, thanks. May God continue to use you for His glory. Amen".*

Well, as I'm fond of saying. "I only use my powers for good!"

CHAPTER 9

Journey Jewels

There is an old saying: "How can two walk together unless they be agreed?" Although such wisdom is often used when considering that "special someone", it is also relevant for those who you choose—or who life chooses—to walk with you.

Such is the case for me . . . Life has afforded me many such walking partners, some who have walked with me in the sunshine and blue skies, whilst others have held my hand to gently guide me back to my path when I didn't, couldn't or wouldn't see the way ahead. Some have run with me, encouraging and coaching, and there have been others who have just enjoyed a pleasant meander for a mile or two. I salute all of you who are my "PPDE's"—Platinum-Plated, Diamond-Encrusted journey jewels! So to all who've walked with me, cried with me and laughed with me (and at me as well!) this is for y'all! We've been walking together since childhood until now and I publicly acknowledge all my PPDE Journey Jewels for allowing the light of their love and friendship to guide me thus far.

In the midst of such brilliance, I want to draw your attention to an extra sparkle, a deeper shimmer and an alluring twinkle of two precious jewels whose light has been a guiding light in my midnight walks of despair, low self-esteem and depression. Thank you both for your love.

DeeDee—My Spirit Sista

I proudly present and introduce DD, my "Spirit Sista". Let me explain what I mean by "Spirit Sista". I really believe that before we were physically born, we were spirits who played together and knew each other in the spirit realm. Okay, I have no proof it happened like that but it makes sense to me—and you can't prove it didn't happen either! I believe we sat on God's lap, where we were held and nurtured by Him and that we even clung to His legs when we saw Him, because isn't that what children do who love and are loved? So when the time came for us to be "released", our instructions were to find each other, as that would help us to invariably find Him.

DD "found" me on my journey at a time when my spirit had been crying out for a sister, someone special I could call my own. I recall writing a poem when I was 14/15 years old, in which I said I wanted a family of my own: a loving father, sisters and brothers. I am sure God must have smiled at the request because little did I know what was to come!

A few years later I received an airmail letter, with a South American post stamp which was to change my life—for ever! DD had written to me, introducing herself as my sister! It was a mind-numbing, heart pulsating moment as I read and read her letter, and the reality of it all just engulfed me. I had a sister, a real-life sister, someone like me, a bonafide flesh and blood sister; not a family friend, a church sister or someone who I hung out with and would maybe take pity on me and give me some remnants of sista-love, but my own, my very own *little* sister . . . ! Now who says God doesn't answer prayers!

I took courage and with mixed emotions—bewilderment, excitement, fear and anticipation—I showed Mum the letter and asked it if was true; if I really had a sister. Mum confirmed the uniqueness and validity of the relationship, explaining that DD and I both had the same biological progenitor (the term "father" is too strong a term for me to use). To give a brief background about "our dad", we never grew up with him as a positive or permanent fixture in our lives, as the circumstances and dysfunctional situation at the time meant our family structure was somewhat different from that of other "normal" families. Yet, I do believe the little time we did have with him as babies, impacted us at an early age and left a lasting impression on our developing years.

When Mum confirmed the reality of the letter, I was silent for what seemed a lifetime, but which was in truth but a moment's silence. After the initial shock, the floodgates opened as Mum began to reminisce and fill me in on this vital missing segment of my life. Apparently, DD and I were practically twins! Born the same year, same month and literally hours apart—but at least I can testify that I am the eldest!

Journey Pause: *Please note: in the sharing of such personal and sensitive information, I am not passing, nor encouraging anyone to pass judgement on situations and affairs of which my sister and I were the result. I have lived long enough to realise I dare not point the finger and seek to judge matters about which I know nothing. Neither DD nor I were in our parents shoes; we could never understand the dynamics of their individual and collective lives nor the emotions and needs which caused them to reach out to each other on such a deep intimate level . . .*

However, there was one experience Mum shared with me which resonated in my spirit, and still does. Dad was a property landlord and I can only guess that, on hearing his burgeoning clan was about to be expanded, he graciously allowed both women a room in one of his properties. (I can't even dare to think about the home arrangements, the tensions and undercurrents they were all living in at the time). Apparently, when our Dad would come home DD would give me the signal (via baby-talk, of course), and I would answer by bouncing down the stairs like a true commando-baby. Thank heavens for old-fashioned terry nappies, as I don't think today's versions could have stood the pace! On arrival, we would launch a full scaled attack on our Dad with DD holding one leg and me the other. Once we latched onto him, we were not letting go! Mum shared how she'd chuckle at the sight memory of him trying to desperately free himself from our childish love assault while crying out "Oh gosh man, lemme go, lemme go!". Yet, he never really seemed in a hurry to dislodge himself from our assault, which according to Mum, was a great source of amusement to us. Looking back, maybe I guess it was, the time we ever really "spent" with him, because he was a man who worked—hard—and was therefore hardly at home. Whenever I remember the story, it always brings tears to my eyes, because it explains so much within me; of the longing of two little girls struggling to hold onto the one who should have been holding onto them, but away with the tears, this is really a happy story!

DD & I seemed to have had a special bond from birth and, dare I say, beyond. Mum recalls whenever DD would be crying, a talent she seemed to excel in at the time, but which of late I seem to be making my own, her Mum would call me and speak to DD in her native Guyanese Creole dialect "Hey girl, DD, look Shalisa! Look, she nah cry, so is why you crying?" and the joke was, I would talk to DD in baby-talk . . . and she would stop! Oh, the power of being the bigger sister, ha ha ha! Remember, we were mere babes at the time, just perfecting the art of babyhood and toddlerism. However, the living situation soon became untenable, as the introduction of one of Dad's girlfriends (who later became his last wife, literally . . .), caused DD and her Mum to relocate to South America. I did not remember or ever recall I had a sister until much, much later . . . when I received her letter. You know, there are times when a letter, a phone call or a visit can change your life—and I am truly grateful for the day DD's letter arrived because my life has never been the same . . .

After much correspondence (and my coming to terms with the shock of it all!), DD returned back home to London in the late 80's. After we spoke on the phone, she agreed to meet me at my local church; maybe we thought such a momentous meeting should be held on "hallowed ground", I don't know! Anyway, the day arrived and so did she. I was astounded this beautiful, slim, young lady was my sister, my very own lil' sis! You can imagine how her arrival really stirred up the gospel gossip columnists and those who were only to happy to offer their services as heir-hunters. Only they were searching for a little more news to discuss and dissect at afternoon tea.

Journey Pause: *I need to just stop here at this point, to recognise and acknowledge the strength and dignity my Mum showed during this time. Not only did she welcome and embrace DD as her own, but she stood with grace and fortitude at a time when tongues were wagging and making up what they didn't know—or would ever be told! I had many people asking the same questions in different ways, rather like a bunch of over-eager lawyers, to see if they could get to the root of who and where we came from—and belonged to. Why they would have wanted or even needed such information is truly beyond me—but hey, such is life.*

DD was—and is—a constant positive blessing in my life. She re-entered my life at a time when I was on a self-destruct programme. For in all my shenanigans, my unfruitful and unsavoury trysts, my emotional rollercoaster rides, DD has been a constant in my life. Her prayers, her understanding, her timely silences (well, not all the time, but she tried), her loving rebukes and above all her unconditional love, all served to keep and navigate me through many a stormy period in my life. DD was my protector and defender in my many hit-and-miss relationships. When "Polyphemous", a guy I was seeing at the time, was messing me around and causing serious heartache, DD devised a classic pay-back. Don't worry it was all legal and above board, but boy, it sure felt good to have someone in my corner! She fought my self-imposed battles and slowly but surely helped to turn me around from the self-destructive path I was on. Not drugs or alcohol but the slow, inner-death of multiple relationships, one-night stands all covered up in a "do-I-care" attitude.

DD often regaled me with stories about her life in S. America and the freedom of growing up in a society where you knew who you, were without having to have government workshops and "positive action" to help you along and where you were able to define and know yourself. I admit I was somewhat envious of her self-awareness, her independence and the fact she really knew her worth. By observation, I learned from DD the art of being assertive: because Caribbean self-awareness and "Black British" self-awareness are two different concepts and I know which one I prefer! Imagine coming from an environment where everyone looks like you, speaks like you, eats like you, understands your culture. A place where "top-class" professions are held by those of your own hue, colour and race. So why wouldn't you think and believe you can and ought to make it? Now imagine relocating to your birthplace, into an environment where subtle and subliminal messages tell you that you are only allowed thus far and no higher. Where jobs and life opportunities are withheld by a society which ironically talks about "better integration" but ensures there are so many hurdles to cross before you can even come close. A society where you're covertly encouraged to "dumb down" in order to fit the status quo . . . Well, that is what my sister faced and knowing who she was and the society she'd just left behind, it was hard for her to accept a notion of expected to fail, when you have seen success stories all your life. DD's life experiences, coupled with my Mum's tales, have all helped inspire and encourage me to continue to move on up.

When DD arrived, we spent many weekends together, literally talking through the night, because we had so many years to catch up on. The fact DD and I were also members of the same denomination also helped our relationship, as we had common ground on which to relate and build on. Whilst I was content to play the "honest hypocrite", with one foot in church and the rest of me outside doing "mah thang", DD's mindset was to walk the talk and boy, was she straight. No, she was not a dry Christian, those people who always look as if they're sucking lemons, nor was she strait-laced. Rather, she was what I was struggling to be. Don't get me wrong; I really tried, but my walk and inner mindset were somewhat crooked and my talk was rather quiet . . .

Journey Pause: *Let me just explain the rationale behind how I termed myself, an "honest hypocrite". As a church-goer, I was subject to and very much aware of the unspoken but powerful 11th commandment: "Thou shalt not get caught". Many of the older folks had—and were still doing—bad, but they'd learned to ensure the 11th commandment was never broken. Domestic, emotional and, I dare say, sexual abuse was acceptable—as long as you didn't get caught and/or knew how to cover it up, which a lot of sistas knew to do—very well. I've heard numerous anecdotes of men preaching the Word with vigour and fire, who'd then go home to beat up their wives. Men, shouting the loudest "amen", who only hours earlier had thrown out their wives' belongings on the street, and were sitting next to their unsuspecting spouse. Saved and holier-than-thou men, who'd play the piano and organ with sanctimonious stature, only to find themselves playing another sweet music on another man's wife—and those are the mere snippets of what I got to hear about! So in my books, being an honest hypocrite meant I had made up my mind to do what I had to do, and not bother to hide it. Unfortunately, unlike my other friends who were brave enough to leave church, I was scared of divine retribution, wagging tongues and finger pointing, I figured I could have enough religion to be saved but enough world to be "baaad!" Looking at women who were at the age at which I now am (gulp), who unmarried, no man, no make-up, no style, and I purposed in my heart that I was NOT going to be dry nor thirsty, when so*

*much water was around me. (I'd just discovered the sweetness of life by
then and yes, that really was my mindset, my modus operandi!) So I knew
if I did what I did, I'd not bother to hide nor deny it but just get on with
it—live everyone else—and ensure the 11th commandment was never
broken. Here endeth my definition of being an "honest hypocrite".*

Oh, the times we had! Camp meetings, church conventions, where we'd
listen to the sermon whilst laughing at the saints and pointing out the
sinners! We often reminisce on those times spent laughing at sayings
and happenings during the sermon and we were very good at giving
people names, a type of "re-christening", if you please! No church was
safe—from south to north, east to west, you could count on use to always
find something—and someone—to amuse us.

In one south London church, we duly renamed the choir director as
"Listen". How that came about was, one day, being both choir director and
lead singer for that particular song, he grabbed hold of the microphone
in a moment of musical ecstasy, closed his eyes and in the break between
verse and chorus shouted "LISTEN!". Now, who told him to say that,
with my sister and I there? As a line in the song "I Will Survive" aptly
states "It took all the strength I had not to fall apart"!! Honestly, it's a
wonder we weren't asked to leave, but such was our story and situation.
Even today, we have to ability to see (and laugh) at those things others
tend to miss and overlook! Another time, which funnily enough was in the
same church (I don't know what it was about those southern churches!),
we were invited to a post-service lunch, at a member's house. In those
days, a lunch invitation was usually a mammoth food-fest and this was
no different. After the various vegetarian, meat, fish dishes, if you still
had room, there was always the golden promise of dessert—and who
isn't able to find or make room for a little apple pie and ice-cream?

On arrival, DD & I found ourselves amidst the crème de la crème of
church society and I admit I felt slightly awed by being in the presence
of such esteemed and august personages. It was hard to resist not asking
for their autographs or if we could take a picture with them, which is to
tell you how "high up" they were. When suddenly, in the midst of such a
grand and dignified gathering, I heard an unbelievable and unexpected
sound—a frenzied scrapping of spoon on bowl! Now, the gentleman

in question was chatting to a young lady who was sitting demurely whilst he was (probably) beguiling her with the latest revelation and philosophy of the time, when in his haste and possibly nervousness (it could never be greed, surely not!), he obviously forgot he was not at home! I have never heard a spoon and bowl go at like that! The apple-pie and ice cream had long since disappeared, but he seemed determined to relive and extend the memory. In between sentences, he scrapped and scrapped and scrapped the bowl. Not silently, I might add; oh no! His was a musical rendition (and yes, he was related to "Listen", so maybe that explains a lot!). It was all we could do not to "buss out" laughing! It's a wonder the bowl remained intact and this is yet another story we still chuckle over even today and yes, I'm sure you can guess what *his* name then became: yes, you got it—he was duly christened "Bowl Scrapper". We referred to him as such, to the point where I don't think we can even remember his real name.

DD and I were (and still are) very good at covering our tracks when in situations where the obviously too funny moments cannot be contained or concealed and we just have to laugh. If cornered and put on the spot, we're now adept in giving a somewhat intelligible garbled message about some other thing, thus helping to cover our tracks and ensure no one is unduly embarrassed, after which we can return checking out the situation in hand.

However, there were also times of deep darkness, when DD's words, presence and unconditional love helped to steer me, keep me and just hold me. Those times when loneliness, despair and depression would surround and overwhelm me and I couldn't and wasn't able to shake them off, it was then DD would miraculously phone me at such appropriate times to listen to me and to pray with and for me. If you have you ever had someone pray for you, then you can understand the sense of relief and joy at hearing someone else voice those words your heart is unable or even unwilling to utter.

Once, during one of our marathon phone calls, which are legendary, DD said " . . . Shalisa, anyone looking at you would never realise that you sometimes suffer from depression and can be so low". Like most women who'd been beaten and bruised from life, I was always able to hide behind a "oh, nothing is wrong, I'm just a natural joker" face (does this sound familiar to anyone out there?). Thankfully DD was, and still is, always able to see through my façade of superficial glitz, empty laughter and a pseudo happy-go-lucky stance—to the real me, the quiet me.

Oh, and while at this point in my journey, please allow me the opportunity to set the record straight: I am the quiet one and DD isn't! A recent case when DD was there for me, was when a recent event, a major journey crash, nearly took me out (*see "Pandora's Box".)*

From My Heart . . . to Yours

DD, there are a multitude of things I wish I could say right now, to convey how much you mean to me, as a spirit-sister and as a friend—but time and words do not permit me. I also realise the depth of feeling between sisters is something that can only be felt, intuitively, and not expressed in a few words, but I take this opportunity to thank you for finding me, for caring for me—and for loving me in spite of me. Thank you for all the late night drama and early morning hysterics you walked me through; thank you for holding my hand (literally!) through many tests and trials. Even though you did not always understand how and why I did what I did (nor with whom I did it), you loved me nonetheless. I thank you for your objectivity. Not because I am your sister, have you ever allowed me to "slip and slide"—far from it! I believe your innate sense of our divine mission enabled you to continually encourage me to keep on stepping up to the mark of our higher calling, as well as to fulfil my personal goal to "be the best me that I can be". Lil' sista, I really appreciate your prayers and your tears which have covered and helped me to remain focused and to keep on my journey.

Still, it's unfair to paint a picture of my always leaning on you; for ours is truly a balanced walk and there have been many times when the tables were turned and I was the one with a listening ear, a concerned heart—and outstretched arms. I believe my ability to comfort, encourage and be a good listener and counsellor is because you taught me well by showing me what and how to do it. From north to south, Guyana and London, from broken hearts and unfulfilled promises, from pregnancy to marriage—and beyond—DD, we can truly say we have come this far by faith—and with a whole lotta laughter!

DD, you have your own journey to walk and I know it's not an easy road, but I really do thank God for assigning us to each other and for orchestrating and allowing our paths to cross, not just at birth, but in so many tangible and meaningful ways. I am blessed to have such a beautiful, strong, sassy and courageous woman of God in my life. I think every woman should seek to find and celebrate their own "spirit-sister". I know I have and welcome this opportunity to showcase a pristine PPDE—platinum-plated and diamond encrusted jewel!

AA

One of my "journey jewels" is AA, life long friend and "partner-in-crime, someone who is Ying to my Yang (or is it the other way round.!). When I first considered what to say about our friendship thus far, I was temporarily stumped. Not because I don't have anything to say, far from it; but because I have too much to say! How can you describe someone with whom you have developed your own language? How can you describe someone who with one hug (& AA is a great hugger!) can impart life, love and hope in that one gesture? How can you describe someone who's life choices may have infuriated you in the short term but who has been a source of inspiration in the long term? How can you describe someone who is one of the few persons to know all about you, sordid details and all, and still love you, regardless? How can you describe someone whose idea of friendship is lifelong, bordering on the eternal, because when AA takes you as a friend, you really have no choice but to go along with the programme because believe me, you **will** be a friend and get treated as one, whether you want it or not! Still, I'm going to try, so here goes.

In the words of a song which says "through many dangers, toils and snares", my friend has lived a life of ups and downs, swings and roundabouts yet retained an air of elegance and grace all of her own. I am blessed to have an honest friend, a trustworthy friend and a loving friend who has walked with me thus far on my journey. At times, our paths have intertwined as we shared similar experiences, cried and laughed together. I believe some friendships are made in heaven and I thank God for this one.

Along our journey, we have not always agreed with what the other has done, but we have stood by and for each other. When travelling life's journey, although you have to walk your own path yourself, it is a blessing to have a helping hand to hold, a listening ear to speak into and a heart to feel with you; other wise it can be a lonely and bitter walk. Now . . . I'm sure that, along your own journey, you have heard the saying "people come into your life for a reason, a season and a lifetime". I now know that some people come into your life like an undercover CIA or MI5 covert with one mission and assignment—to help keep you on the straight and narrow and in the uncovering your purpose and destiny.

It's amazing how we've worked and walked out our friendship; we swing our arms together and often match each other's marching step yet we're as individual as we can be. Even if we buy the same outfit and shoes, we are close enough to have similar tastes yet be individual to wear them in our own unique and distinctive style. Shoes . . . hmmm! Did I tell you we like shoes, no, really, we *like* shoes big time; trust me, it's great to have someone with a like passion. We only have to hear the word "shoes" and we both look at each other, with a glazed and hungry look in our eyes; maybe we should set up a "Shoe Anonymous" meeting, with a 12-step programme (pardon the pun!) Listen: we can describe a shoe in such detail to each other, that the other person can literally see and feel it on their foot, that's how bad we got it! In fact, we've been able to "dress" each other over the phone (don't ask!) because we have a general idea of what is in each other's closet . . . skeletons and all, hahahaha! There are sooo many instances I'd love to share, but knowing AA's quest for privacy, I'll make sure the spotlight isn't too much in her face . . . ! In sharing my journey, the following is an experience I had with AA when we had our first holiday together . . . as friends . . . (Did our friendship last? Just you wait and see . . . !)

I will start with the first time we went on holiday together. Now, friends and life-long couples know such a venture can really break or make a friendship or relationship. Yes, we'd done the stay over, the long, long, LONG chats about boyfriends, clothes, shoes, boys and back to shoes again but this time, we'd decided to take a break. At the time, AA was a young mother of three which I kept forgetting; in fact, her offspring were a welcome addition but I often forget the maternal instinct to stay and brood over one's . . . brood, I guess. I guess AA can well lay claim to being one of the original "Yummy Mummy's", because she always, ALWAYS looked good (& still does!).

Well, after much debate on destination and persuasion on my part, oh and having to make the necessary childcare arrangements, because remember, I was footloose and fancy-free; my "care responsibilities" were usually summed up as "Mum! I've gone! See you later!" followed by a loving "mwah" as I'd plant a loving but hurried kiss on her cheek, we agreed to go to Tunisia. I'd gone there before, once with Mum in 1994 and then on my own in 1995 to "get away" and to celebrate a major birthday.

Journey Pause: *By the way, I'm a staunch believer in celebrating one's birthday, especially mine, because if God took time to make you and Mother Nature took time shape you, you just gotta be worth a little cake and a whole lot of T.L.C.!*

In 1995 I'd met a wonderful Tunisian on the last day of my holiday there. He was one of the local tour guides and somehow we "clicked". Maybe it was because I was far from home; maybe it was because he hailed from the fatherland (aka the African continent) or maybe it was the sultry atmosphere, the Tunisian spices and the hot and spicy harissa . . . Whatever it was, our trip proved to be an "interesting" milestone in my journey, one which AA would be privy to—up close and personal.

Fast forward to 1996; young, fresh and keen we headed to Tunisia. Now, having been there twice already, I was no longer a tourist. Oh no, I was a seasoned traveller and a tourist expert in all things Tunisian. (You know those people who go to a place a couple of times and come back more knowledgeable than the natives). So, armed with a few choice words of Arabic and my innate sense to lead, we were off! Well, the first hurdle happened before we even left the house. As a veteran traveller, I could able to pack a mean case with all my essentials in a mini hold-all, but

AA, in her excitement to ensure she did not want for anything, could barely close her suitcase. After removing shoes (yes, they were the main culprits) and a few non-essentials, we were ready. Bearing in mind we were going for just one week and would be spending most of it with my Tunisian friend (opps, did I forget to add that minor detail?), AA felt the need to take a little of everything, which in her case, added up to a lot. But we would not let such a simple thing as an overflowing suitcase defeat us; no way!

Journey Pause: *Ahh, it all comes flooding back! I had gone to Tunisia on my own and on my last day there, I met my Tunisian friend. Absolutely gorgeous—or maybe it was the sun, the atmosphere and just enjoying a much needed break alone. When he approached me, I was flattered but cautious, yet I obviously threw caution to the wind when I told him which hotel I was staying at. (I also think I was a little reckless as I knew I was leaving the next morning!). He met me at my hotel for a drink, where we laughed and talked together. We hugged, swapped contact details and he promised to keep in touch, and I went up to my room . . . happy and alone. We kept in touch and I could see myself, a Nubian princess with my very own Lawrence of Arabia . . . sigh . . . !*

Once we'd conquered the suitcase by emptying, repacking and practically sitting on it, at last, we were on our way. Now, AA knew all about my Tunisian "friend" and had agreed to spend our first night in Tunisia Hammamet and the remainder of the time at with my friend. I was very vocal in proclaiming to AA that yes, of course she and I would be sharing the same room, because we were *not* that type of girl! But oh, how the mighty are fallen!

It was when we boarded the Air France plane, our fun really started! Trust me when I tell you, AA and I always ride shotgun for each other! For a start, we thought we had enough time to get something to eat before we boarded the plane. I mean, it was only a short flight and we didn't know if lunch was provided and hey, London divas need to eat too! So we had a Mickey D breakfast, pancakes and all! So while munching and enjoying the pre-holiday excitement, we began to notice the eating area was somewhat empty; where was everybody? We then saw a man running like crazy to one of the boarding gates. I don't know why it alerted us to get up "just in case" and decide to follow him. Good thing we did, as he was heading for the same flight which was practically about to take off! With the remnants of our Mickey D breakfast, we made a mad dash and got to the plane with minutes to spare. When we stepped in and look at row after row of our fellow passengers, we noticed we were the only "flies in the milk". (For those who don't understand and for the politically minded, it means we were the only "visible ethnic minorities" on the plane—well, as far as we could see). Don't misunderstand me, as having been born and raised in London, you get used to sometimes being the "jewel in the crown", so to speak, but when in a confined space and on a foreign plane, trust me, it was very hard to miss. Plus, the fact we were the last ones to arrive and giggling to boot, I guess just made us stand out a just a wee bit more than usual.

Having found our seats, we finished off the rest of our breakfast (like I said—we street-wise divas we hungry!) but about 20 mins after take-off, the air-hostess came round with a breakfast tray and being of the "waste-not-want-not" school of life, we accepted—and ate—with a glad heart and a full tummy. Now, not sure of exactly where we would be staying in Tunisia nor of the living arrangements, we both agreed it made sense to keep the cutlery provided; after all, we're very resourceful. However, being the only flies on a non-English speaking plane made such actions very difficult to hide! The passenger next to us was saying:

> "Je pense que vous devriez le remettre! Les couverts ne sont pas en plastique; ils sont métal et seront sélectionnés vers le haut de quand vous passez par la sécurité!" (I think you should put it back! The cutlery is not plastic; they are metal and will be picked up when you go through security!)"

Now, to a French person, it would obviously make sense; you don't want to be arrested as a suspected terrorist because of the airline's "forchette", but when the warning is given in French and you are English—you can imagine it's not going to be heeded at best and laughed at, at worst! AA and I tried to hide our giggles but my snorts of laughter gave the game away; we just found the whole thing absolutely hilarious! By then, the passenger had raised her voice and had probably added a few more choice adjectives, thankfully unbeknown to us, because by then all other passengers were glaring at us, which only made the joke more delicious. In between the side-splitting laughter (honestly, you had to be there to appreciate the sweetness of it all!), we managed to get the gist of what she was saying because, coupled with the warning were several Gaelic hand gestures and facial expressions and so we reluctantly removed the cutlery from our handbags.

It is just as well we did, because on arrival at the airport, we were heavily searched by the well-armed airport security (I'm sure someone had given a Gaelic whisper or two). But hey, we didn't mind: we were on our way to Tunisia and nothing absolutely nothing, was going to spoil our fun! We arrived at the Bel Air Hotel and enjoyed the high life, a welcome respite after all the travelling trauma we'd just experienced. Ahh, now we were truly on holiday, this was the life—a lovely hotel, good food and mediocre hotel entertainment meant we were set for the next phase of our holiday.

Now, I had arranged for us to spend the rest of the holiday with my "Tunisian pen pal", because at the time, I thought "I was woman; watch me roaaar!", and was equipped, and well able to handle anything life could throw at me. Well, I went from being a roaring lion to a little meowing cat, believe you me! I was looking forward to meeting my international beau, Mr Tunisia, and to introducing him to my good friend. (You know how we sistas like to do it! We have to check out each other's prospective beau and give them the once over to see if they're okay for our friend). But it's a shame when the rose-coloured description doesn't always seem to match up to the reality when you finally get to introduce the person to your best friend, and you begin to see things from a more objective perspective.

Now, when I had first met him, Mr Tunisia was tall, golden brown, with Tunisian sunshine, olive oil and a Mediterranean tan to match. On meeting him, he had shrunk and was now a little taller than me, with a bald patch and a moustache. How I missed the bald patch, I just don't know. Maybe it was the sunlight glinting on the olive-oil smooth surface which dazzled me, which distracted me or made me think he had a permanent halo. And while I'm not averse to a little face design, a full blown moustache isn't really my thing.

AA had listened to my stories of love in the Tunisian sun, sand and sea (honestly, all we did was have a cup of coffee in the hotel bar!) but to my romantic mind, it was a sign—he was the One. Now, on the way to Tunisia and before Mr T was coming to get us, I (as usual) was speaking with authority: "AA! Listen, I am sharing a room with you! I don't know what kind of girl he thinks I am, but I didn't come out here to get up to anything. Oh no, that's not me". I can now understand why AA just listened with a wry smile on her face. I seem to have an unenviable talent of speaking the very opposite of what is about to happen to me. In my mind, it was all so simple. If and when he was to ask me where I'd be sleeping, I had a speech ready and waiting for him. I was going to rise up to my full 5' 2" stature and boldly and emphatically declare that "oh no, I will NOT be sleeping with him but rather share a room with AA". Yes, I'd even practiced the obligatory dismissive hand-flick I'd use when delivering my speech. Oh have mercy! How the mighty are fallen!

When we reached his apartment away from the tourist trade, in a little town outside Hammamet, we went in and it's then it hit me: I suddenly realized that I had invited my friend, my best friend, to spend a holiday with me and some man I had only just met a few months before. (Why, oh why, can't hindsight come before the event?). So, with a dry mouth and some trepidation, we went inside, where the next events seemed to happen so fast yet in painfully slow motion. Mr Tunisia duly carried our suitcases upstairs and placed AA's in *her* room but when I looked in the room to see where my case was, it wasn't there.

"Erm, Mr T, did you bring my case up? It's not in AA's room?"

The answer came back in honeyed tones with Tunisian olive oil saturating it: "No, it's here in my room."

What?!! I nearly died with shame! He wasn't following the script! He was supposed to *ask* me where I wanted to sleep and then, and then, I would deliver my speech and . . . it wasn't far for him to assume be with him! And furthermore how could I possibly share a room, a *bedroom* with a man—*and* know my best friend was in the same house—at the same time! Now, I know this is hardly the stuff of scandal nowadays but back then and for who we were (or at least were trying to be), for me it was the height of embarrassment! I was practically at the top of the scale! When Mr Tunisia just laid down the law, AA later said I silently shuffled, head bowed into his room.

Journey Pause: *Even as I write, I just feel sooo embarrassed. Why? Because even though AA & I would talk about relationships and all that happened—to a certain degree—it was another thing to your friend witness it up close and personal. I also felt cowed into submission because I just felt I really didn't have a leg to stand on. Now, it'd be a different situation! I, we, wouldn't be in such predicament in the first place and, knowing who I now am and Who I belong to would NOT find me there. But remember, along life's journey, we all have "fallen and come short".*

Well sista, I will leave this experience here at this point because there are some journeys that one has to walk alone, painful and shameful though it may be. Suffice to say, night time found me sleeping with eyes wide open as I was too afraid to breathe too hard. Let me just stop right here, as I'm blushing even as I write this, have mercy!

So why share this holiday experience? Because it stands out in my mind as a classic example of AA's non-judgmental attitude, for not once did AA use this—or any of my other many misdemeanours—against me. She never judged me (although she did later admit to guffawing about the whole situation, especially since I'd been piously and boldly declaring it to be a chaste and innocent holiday).

Another Tunisian anecdote we still laugh about from that holiday was when I was struggling to close my suitcase.

Now, there's something about me and holidays, where I feel the need to cram as much of the experience into my suitcase (literally) before I return home and this was no exception. With what seemed to be half of Tunisia in my luggage, I begged, cried, cajoled and finally sat on it (honestly!) before I was able to lock it up. As I stood up to proudly survey my victory and the now fit-to-burst suitcase, I loudly proclaimed "Well done, my son!", only to nearly jump out of my skin as AA flung open the door and burst into the room in fits of laughter! Apparently, as she was going by, she said all she could hear was heavy breathing, groaning and grunting, and whispers: "that's it, you're in and don't you dare come out" and the final straw of "well done my son" was a step too far for her and she wanted to know *who* I was talking to, especially as Mr. T wasn't at home! Ever since then, "well done, my son" can literally reduce us to tears!

Since then, we've shared several holidays; the last one where I nearly didn't come back home . . . but that is another story, for another book! Together, we have searched for oil in Miami, shopped till we dropped in New York and enjoyed carnival in Castries, and each time, it has been such a blessing to share my journey with a really good, true and honest friend. Difference of opinions? Nah, we both love shopping, shoes and handbags, so tell me, what *is* there to ever differ about, hahaha?!! Over the years, we have opened up and have shared our hurts, pains joys and laughter with each other. We have supported each other through thick and thin along our individual and joint journey.

My Hospital Visitor

It's not often that I'm sick but when I am, it feels as if my life is over. Like most people, I hate feeling so vulnerable and having to go to hospital for a minor operation made it even worse. I casually let slip I was going in but that " . . . I'd be alright; nothing to worry about". AA, being AA, investigated the procedure and warned me recovery would be painful but no, not for me, Ms Hercules-I-feel-no-pain Shalisa!! The day of the operation came and I set off, intending to be safely home and tucked in my bed, later that night. When AA asked how I was going to get home and I casually replied that I'd take to a cab, to which suggestion she just laughed as if to say "Huh, we'll see".

Well, after the operation (which obviously went well because I'm still here!), I was in the recovery room. As it when coming round after anaesthetic, the mind tends to kick in before the body has a chance to come round. I lay there, just amazed at how the process of waking up when I didn't even remember going off to sleep! I remember getting ready to gingerly swing my legs off the bed to stand up (because remember, I was going home that night!) when the pain just hit me, POW!, in my stomach.

If felt as if Mike "Iron" Tyson had decided to use my abdomen for target practice; honestly, it was not good, not good at all. A nurse asked if I was able to walk to the bathroom and before I could answer, she dropped a bombshell, which was almost as bad as the pain in my stomach, and told me that if I was in too much pain, I would have to spend the night in the hospital. Her comment spurred me on to grit my teeth, ignore the throbbing, hot pains shooting through me and I managed to painfully and slowly shuffle to the bathroom. On the way there, I passed a fellow patient coming back from the bathroom, who had to be held up by two (TWO!) people in order to get back to the ward. The fact she was crying and moaning did not make me feel any better about my situation, and of course my own pains just seemed to intensify at that point.

Have you ever prayed to go the bathroom, you know, to *go to the loo*? Well, when it was my turn, I had to do just that, because I truly believe God is with you in part of your life journey experience, even in a hospital bathroom! My prayer was "Lord, I really need to go without any pain, because I really do not want to spend the night here!" and who said He doesn't hear? The answer was instantaneous and like the shower from Niagara Falls on a summer's day, the relief was . . . ohhhh! I eventually managed to shuffle back to my bed and seemed to impress the hospital staff enough to release me, although I was gritting my teeth and trying to smile through the pain. I was slowly and painfully getting dressed and thinking about how and where I'd be able to call a cab—who should appear but AA! What a gal! I was so touched, because, deep down, I really needed someone to be with me but just didn't know who or even how to ask for help—even though help had been offered . . .

Journey pause: *Isn't this one of life's traps that we all fall into every now and then? I'd like to take this opportunity to explode the myth of the SBW (strong, Black woman); she doesn't exist!! It's just ploy to get us to keep going . . . and going . . . and going, until we drop. We ain't anymore "stronger" than any other woman; indeed, if that's the case, then ALL women are strong, irrespective of race, colour &/or creed! No, the SBW myth originated in part from slavery, and was furthered engineered and promoted to ensure the female of the species was always ready and prepared to take on the woes and worries of others, often at the expense of her needs. How many of us, especially our "sistas of colour", refuse* *to take "time out", without being made to feel like a failure—and it's usually our voice which is the loudest accuser. Sista, that was me, the quintessential SBW, when at the time and indeed, all along, I was weak and vulnerable and someone to help me . . .*

AA helped me to finish getting dressed and walked me out to the car. Yet, even in a stage of post-operative pain, I remember saying "Oh AA, I'm alright you know! You really didn't have to come from so far to take me home" (she lives outside of London and to where the hospital was, was not a short drive). I remember sitting in the car, just so glad to have a sista-girlfriend that I could just be myself with; someone I could relax with and take off the "SBW" (strong Black woman) mask which we force ourselves to wear.

Journey pause: *Let's be honest; it's not many people we dare unmask ourselves to, because although we say may be friends, we really don't want to be the one to put it to the test, just in case it fails. In case our friend cannot take the real us, our inner self, the part of us which we are still struggling to come to terms with. Is it that, in finding it hard to be honest with ourselves, we therefore find it hard to be honest with others, even those we claim to be our loved ones and friends? When are we ever without our masks? When can we just stop and cry out, knowing there is a safe haven, a comfort inn, a hiding place where we can stop and refresh ourselves and get nourishment, "soul" food? Even when we're down and out, wounded and weary, many a woman, (and not just those of SBW variety either), can be heard to say "Oh, I'm alright, it's nothing!". All we are doing is teaching others how to react and to treat us. We ourselves are solely responsible for setting boundaries for a cycle of behaviour, which only serves to keep where we are. It's time for us to be honest with ourselves—and learn to love ourselves enough to allow others to love us—as we are . . . .*

I learned a valuable lesson from that experience: AA truly has my back . . . and for that, I am grateful. Now, before I end this chapter, don't think it's all one-sided—I'm there for her too and have often been "Thelma" to her "Louise!".

Sistas—remember this: when you're a "giver", you need to recognize and admit the need that YOU also need to receive . . . .

From My Heart . . . to Yours

AA, through many dangers, toils and snares we have walked with each other along our respective paths. Sometimes side-by-side, sometimes along a lonely path, yet we have always been there to cheer each other on, to shout encouragement and warnings from the sidelines. We've often jumped in to fight each others' battles and yet we know when to step back from the fray if it's obvious we're in danger of crossing the line. Underlying everything is our love for one another and the respect it brings. For we treasure our individuality whilst being able to celebrate our similarities. Girlfriend, we've come this far by faith and I look forward to the next phase of my journey with my PPDE to help light my way and lighten the load!

CHAPTER 10

There But for Grace . . . .

There but for the grace of God . . . go I.

In the sharing of my journey so far, I've highlighted some key moments, experiences, situations and incidents where, had it not been for Someone walking with me and watching my back, I really would not be here. These flashbacks and momentary dips into the past help to keep me humble as it's hard to point an accusatory and judgmental finger at someone else, when three of your own are pointing right back at you (try it and see . . . . aha, told you so!). It was those flashbacks which kept occurring in the writing of other chapters, and served as timely reminders that hey, I really did not and could not have gotten here by myself! For how could I ever manage to have walked such a precarious tight rope and not fall, whilst others, having taken a tentative step or two along their own journey, seemingly fell at the first hurdle? So, put your hand in mine as I walk you through this part of my journey. Be careful now, it's a relative minefield, as buried memories, unspoken feelings and smouldering experiences can detonate and explode at any time. Don't be afraid because "she who walks alone has always walked with One!"

"Mr. T."

Mr. T entered my life in my mid-twenties, fresh, hot and ready, ready, ready from the Caribbean. His manner, his looks, his arrogance, his whole demeanour just mesmerized and captured me—and the plus factor was that he really liked me! We met when my then boyfriend was on holiday and, because he had not written or phoned me for over 6 weeks, I thought we were over.

Journey Pause: *How often on our life's journey do we allow hidden insecurities and inferiority complexes to accompany us along the way and to be our guiding light! When my boyfriend left to go "back home" for a well-deserved break from his studies, I thought, assumed and had imagined that yes, we* were *in a committed relationship. I really did believe him when he said "Babes, of course I'll write you every day", only to find myself self-consciously loitering by the door around the time the post was due to arrive. By the third or fourth week it began to dawn to me that he was just one more from the "say-but-don't-do" school of life—and it hurt, it really did. I know I'm not the first (nor probably the last) woman this has happened to, but whilst I acknowledge that one experience doesn't make a lifetime, you do start to wonder when similar events seem to occur too frequently and you realize that such occurrences can and do have an impact on your perspective of life. In this case, such happenings served to reinforce the very negative outlook I had. I interpreted his not calling or writing me as "Shalisa: you're not worthy; Shalisa: you're a fool for believing and trusting someone else" and so on. Worst of all was dealing with my own self-criticism and mocking, as I played and replayed my part in being too trusting, hopeful and naïve. It's sad and soul destroying when the little voice in your head, which is delightfully pointing out all your foibles and idiosyncrasies, is your own . . . !*

When we first met, Mr T's chat up line which caught me hook, line and sinker was " . . . I'm not interested in your boyfriend, I'm interested in you" (super corny, I know but hey—it worked!). Based on the uniqueness (and cheesiness) of his approach, I agreed to meet him the following day. Our first date was at London Zoo (says it all, doesn't it!), followed by a romantic, hand-in-hand stroll over Tower Bridge, where we ended up in his house—and our illicit affair began. Being the honest "church girl" I was professing (or should I say, pretending) to be, I had to break the news to him and "Sweet B", being new to all things relational, took the road less travelled and agreed to forgive me as long as I stopped seeing Mr. T.

Journey Pause: *Why did I do it? Because back then, I did not understand the "power of a need", a term you'll read about in the following chapter. Mr. T made me feel special, physically attractive and desirable, at a time* *when the person I thought and assumed should have been doing that, seemed to have gone AWOL. I knew it was wrong, but on reflection, I think I'd basically had enough of trying to be a "nice girl", when it looked as if the "bad girls" were having fun and trust me, I wanted to have a lil' fun too! I am not here to trivialise or glamorise this event, but to somehow try to explain to others—and myself—the place I was in, the person I was then and the factors which brought me to that point. A key factor which is often overlooked is the power of choice. For regardless of what I can say, explain, highlight or even try to argue away, at the end of the day it was **my** choice, and for many of us, we have to recognize that cold hard fact about ourselves. On our own journeys, we need to look ourselves squarely in the eye and admit: **We** chose to do it; **we** chose to go there; **we** allowed it to happen to us.*

Now, I've never taken drugs nor been (knowingly) drunk; it's just not my thing but intimacy, and the desire to feel flesh on flesh? Hmmm, that's another story . . . Being with Mr. T wasn't just about sex, which was new, raw and exciting); no, for me, it was something truly kinetic, the synergy of two likeminded persons. I only had to *hear* his voice or just imagine him . . . and that was it for me. Yes sistas, I had it *real* bad for "Mr. T". I promised faithfully, tearfully and with every ounce of my being, to stop seeing Mr T for my boyfriend's sake, because I could see how hurt he was by my behaviour and yes, I did love him, after a fashion. Or at least, what I thought was love at the time because, let's face it, if you love someone, I mean really love someone, you don't actively seek to continuously hurt them—or yourself. I've since come to realize that love is not a feeling, it's a principle. It is not based on how you, he, they, or even "it" as an emotion *feels*, but as a principle, if it is unselfishly followed, it will direct your feelings to go where the "will" goes, and not the other way around.

Journey Pause: *General concepts of the term "principle", define it as a rule or standard especially of good behaviour, a basic truth of law or assumption, a rule of personal conduct. In other words, if you love someone, you would (and should) surely desire the best for them in all areas. To accomplish this, we need to be mindful to engage the will and utilize our freedom of choice. When dealing with affairs of the heart along your own journey, remember that your will is the navigator behind* *all your choices. It should be the will—the desire to do good and to be the best—which is in the driving seat and not our ephemeral, subjective emotions, which are usually reactive as opposed to proactive.*

At the time, I had my first ever car and was independent with a capital "I". Looking back, I think I was probably going through the rebellious teenage years whilst in my early-to-mid-twenties. We would ring each other up and arrange to meet at leafy, green secluded spots to solidify our "love" in my car, after which he'd write his feelings on the misty windows . . . the truth of which often threatened to come back to haunt me.

One memorable time was when Mr. T, my boyfriend and myself were in the car. (How all three of us happened to be in such close proximity, after everything that had happened—and was still happening—was beyond me.) Being a cold day, the car window started misting up, from the engine heat and the heat of the situation we were all in. Suddenly, I heard coughing and stifled laughter from the back as Mr. T surreptitiously pointed out the proverbial writing on the wall, aka the back seat window! Have mercy, Lord, it was all there, the evidence was out in the open for all to see: our love hearts, our feelings, were somehow, still visible on the steamy windows, I mean REALLY visible! I never knew foolishness like that could take so long to dissipate, but hey, that's another lesson I was yet to learn. I nearly crashed the car as I glimpsed our "lurve" writings in the rear view mirror. I casually passed him an old cloth and asked him to get rid of the evidence under the pretext of wiping the windows clear for me. There is an ancient proverb which says " . . . *Stolen waters are sweet, and bread eaten in secret is pleasant*" and yes, the food I was eating was truly sweet and nice " . . . *but little do they know that the dead are there, that her guests are in the depths of the grave"*. Suffice to say, time had yet to reveal I would soon experience the painful reality of that saying.

Journey Pause: *What a timely moment to pause, stop and reflect! Isn't it always the way when, having agreed the journey and navigated the journey details, you're in full throttle, roaring towards your desired destination, when a casual peek in life's rear-view mirror can cause you to become unbalanced at best, and a major road catastrophe at worst! Life has a way of reminding you at the most inopportune and awkward*

times, where you have been and—in my case—what you have done!
It can cause an emotional, relational and even psychological pile up.
So—what do you do? There are never any easy answers but a probable
and indeed, a practical suggestion, would be to always keep on your
eyes on the road ahead! Rear-view mirror driving is not only well-nigh
impossible, but looking back will not take you to where you want to go;
it'll only show you where you have been! So sistas, do not look back,
not matter how tempting or alluring! Keep your eyes on what you want
to achieve and where you have purposed to go and remember—looking
back will do just that: keep you back!

Time went by; we managed to move on but we did not forget each other. Bearing in mind the social circles we moved in, it was hard not to hear snippets and updates about him. Thus I got to know what he was up to, yet still try and pretend I didn't hear or was interested. Even if I didn't ask, the information was always there, like a tempting chocolate bar. But one day, it all changed. The time came when he visited me with news that nearly tore my heart out: he was getting married. He sat down and I was trying (and hopefully succeeding), to appear rather blasé about his being in such close proximity to me and not wanting to touch or hold him . . . After some general chit-chat, he told me the girl he was seeing had gotten pregnant and he was going to marry her. It cut me to the bone. I wanted to tell him "NO, you're doing the wrong thing" and that it "shoulda been me". Yet I swallowed the pain of that moment and all I could ask him was "Are you sure? Are you sure you're doing the right thing? Marrying because your girlfriend is pregnant is not the most stable of foundations. Are you sure you're doing the right thing?"

His responded as if he were trying to reassure both himself as well as me. Yes, they were both in the same church and he saw this situation as a means of changing his "womanizing" ways. He said "for once, Shalisa, I'm trying to do the right thing". Ha, what goes around surely does come around! You see, Mr T met his "future wife" when he and I were on a brief hiatus. Because of how we had met, our relationship was of the "on-off-on-off" variety and so this had happened during our latest "off" phase. We spoke a little bit more about his future and his need to change and do the right, as well as pending wedding plans, then hugged and parted as friends. I knew I should, could and would never see him again.

Little did I know I was about to get a sharp lesson our life and journey experiences were not yet over!

A few months later, an envelope dropped through my door and on opening it, I found I was holding an invitation to Mr. T's wedding! When I told my boyfriend, "Sweet B" (yes, we were still limping along together) he was not too happy about the invitation but recognized that, being the bigger and better person, he and I would go, together. He said he was not threatened as he know how we felt about each other and that our attendance would be an act of solidarity.

Well, Mr T's wedding day finally dawned and there I stood, next to my boyfriend, watching the man I love walk down the aisle to marry another woman. Interesting . . . I smiled with a broken heart and after the wedding, I hugged her feeling like a hypocrite and when I had to congratulate him, I didn't know whether to break down and cry or just grab him and run! It was my boyfriend's gentle hand on my waist which reminded me things had moved on . . . and so should we. At the reception, I sat with my boyfriend and some of Mr. T's cousins at a family table, laughing and joking, although one of his cousins who knew we'd been an item, was aware of the nuances and undercurrents going on. We ate, drank and laughed and I think I was a little hysterical because I just couldn't stop laughing. Indeed, it was a defense mechanism I was to use to good effect later on.

After the usual raft of wedding speeches, Mr. T stood up, and from the way he acted, you'd have thought he was the bride, the star of the show!. He looked around and his eyes lingered just a little bit too long at our table. He started to thank everyone for coming and supporting him on *his* big day and blah, blah, blah. I sat there, toying with the usual wedding knick-knacks on the table, when all off a sudden, I heard: "Now, it could have been someone else here with me today . . . and Shalisa knows who that person is". Have you ever had a moment where time stands still, everything just freezes and you're the only one moving? Where you can walk around and survey everyone and everything in that split second? Well, that was what seemed to happen. I sat there and I didn't feel the heat of shame and the hot flush of embarrassment. Instead, I felt the icy cold from the sharp intake of breath from my boyfriend, the thud of his hands on the table and the scrapping of a cousin's chair from the table, as he too, registered the moment. As everyone started to look for who this "Shalisa" was (I was so embarrassed and ashamed, even I started to look for "Shalisa"!!), but in my mind, I'd removed myself into my own space and place . . . far from the maddening crowd and the intensity of the moment. It kept playing and replaying, over and over and over on the screen in my mind. Mr. T said that! He really said it, not only in front of his family and wedding guests but also in front of his newly-wedded, pregnant wife! My God! After the wedding reception, which thankfully didn't turn into a wedding day showdown, Mr. T then arranged for all family and close friends (ha!) to continue the wedding festivities at his sister's house.

As Sweet B and I drove off, you could have cut the atmosphere with a sledgehammer as he was mad, hurt and humiliated. Me? I just sat there navigating my way, not only from North to East London but also through the maze of messy emotions and feelings threatening to overwhelm me. When we arrived, I nonchalantly walked into the house, but was feeling so low inside, I could have slithered in. I managed to catch up with Mr. T and proceeded to give him a serious tongue-lashing, the polite version being:

> "Mr. T! How could you do that, not only to me, but to your wife? Your wife!?! You know, the woman you just said "I do" too? You know, the woman who is carrying your child?"

> Mr. T just laughed, grabbed me and pulled me into the kitchen to introduce me to his sister (was there no end to this shame fest that I seemed to be embroiled in?) and said "Sis, this is the woman I should have married!"

By then, my Trini blood was boiling and I was getting ready to unleash the full length of my tongue and to let him have it good and proper, no holding back—but Sweet B, Mr. T's cousin were in the sitting room, along with other family and guests who were starting to arrive. I was NOT about to have a "Jerry Springer" moment, but God knows, I was *that* close to it! That has to be the worst wedding ever; we sat there with all our unspoken words being shouted above the polite conversation and general post-wedding banter. How we got home, I don't know. All I know was that I had some serious damage control to take care of—and it wasn't even my fault, because hadn't I left and walked away and done the "right thing"?

Journey pause: Ever had sticky tape sticking to you after the job has finished? You shake it off one finger and it sticks to another; you shake it off that one, and it sticks to your hand . . . and before you know it, you're in a battle with a piece of sticky tape that does not want to let you go! That's how certain relationships are; you want to move on but they don't want to let go! Sistas, if you feel the stick, stick, stickiness of such a situation, don't try to tackle it on your own! Swallow your pride and shout for HELP! Whether it's prayer, praise, a long walk or even just to make the decision to turn and run, try to find a way or someone, to help untangle you and get you out of the mess! Believe me, if you don't—it will only get worse . . .

Fast forward a few months. Mr. T and his wife had a lovely baby boy and were getting on just fine in their marriage. I was foolish enough to think I could forget. I imagined it was really all over between us, because one of my inherent laws included NOT dating or even being remotely involved with, a married man. You see, when Mr. T said "I do", my heart said "I don't". I had to release him and move on—which I did. Sadly but inevitably, the trauma of all that had happened, coupled with other relationship factors, resulted in Sweet B and I separating and agreeing to continue to our own journey—solo.

Journey Pause: *Why oh why, do we always try to hold on to what we need to let go? What is it that keeps us clinging to the past, whether good or bad? What is it in our individual and gender-specific psyches that insist on retaining a piece of the pie—even though we know it's all over? This is an issue I'm sure a lot of women face; trying to move back into 2ⁿᵈ gear when you've been speeding along in a high-octane relationship at over 100 miles an hour; it's well-nigh impossible at best and emotionally disastrous at worst! Why? Because when we try to "just be friends" after having been intimate at the highest level, it's like a hook in your emotions, as well as being unfair to the other person. I now realize that, like a new-born baby, it's best to just cut the cord and let it go . . . .*

I went to see the happy family to congratulate them (now you know that cut like a knife! Not because of any angst against the wife but because of my submerged feelings which I thought had long gone). We engaged in social chitchat and Mr T and I tried to ignore the emotional breakers that seemed to be going on around and within us. I remember (foolishly) thinking, "Yes! I'm over him! I'm actually over him" and I began to relax and enjoy the visit, where I was honestly able to congratulate them on their new addition.

Journey pause: *What you bury will and does grow; what you keep in the dark will and must come out into the light! When you bury, ignore and disregard your own feelings, you leave yourself open to self-deception, for what you thought could be contained will eventually burst through . . . and take it from me when it happens the person most surprised is . . . YOU!*

Reconnection

It was a social church gathering, a major event at a Central London venue which I attended with my Mum and family friends. Mum, for some strange reason, decided to stay on for the afternoon session with her friends and I decided to go back home—alone. I was hungry and tired and the resultant dull headache was threatening to develop into something major. The fact I had just seen Mr. T didn't help, in fact, it only seemed to make it worse and I really just wanted to get away from the place—and my memories—as fast as possible. Bright sunshine welcomed me as I stepped onto the crowded Regent Street pavement to begin making my way to where I had left my car, when I suddenly heard my named called—"Shalisa! Shalisa!" In hindsight, I really should've taken Dionne Warwick's advice to "walk on by" but no, I stopped and, with what I hoped was an air of indifference I turned round to come face to face with . . . Mr. T. It seemed as if it was we were the only people on the pavement, as if everyone else had "zoned" out. At that moment, even though we were appearing to speak indifferently, casually, our body language was having its own conversation. We weren't touching but hey, we really didn't need to. We could speak volumes whilst standing feet apart. He asked me what I was doing and, against my better judgment, I told him I was going home. He wasn't driving at the time and asked me for a lift. I remembered hesitating but chose to ignore the still, small voice of warning because, hey, what could happen now? I was over him! He was married and remember my rule: I DON'T "do" married men, thank you!

We took a black cab to where I had parked the car, because, being Regent's Street, parking space was at a premium and whenever we attended that venue, we'd often have to park a few bus stops away and then walk back. (Why I always remember that fact, I don't know). We hailed black cab to where I'd left my car and I can always see us sitting in the back of the cab . . . alone . . . together. I don't recall how I drove home, but my next definitive memory is arriving home and walking up the stairs to my flat. My every step seemed to echo and reverberate as it was matched by that of Mr. T behind me. I opened the door and it was then that the silence hit me: Mum was not home and I was alone, all alone, with Mr. T. Yet it was still "all good". I had my standards, discipline and principles—I did NOT date married men and there was NO WAY I was going to disappoint myself or let God down.

We sat on the sofa at opposite ends, for "never the twain was to meet" and after the usual hospitalities and formalities, we started talking about the meeting, God and our relationship with Him, when all of a sudden, the atmosphere just changed. There was a shift; you could feel it; it really was an electrical moment. Now, no one had moved (because I know I certainly hadn't); he was still sitting where he was, at the other end of the sofa, but all of a sudden, it felt like rain was about to fall; the air began to feel heavy and oppressive as submerged feelings, anticipations and desires began to reawaken and arise. I began to recognise the growing surge of long buried feelings and emotions and suddenly realized—you know what, Mr. T. HAS to go.!

I jumped up and said, with as much strength as I could (because remember, I'm fighting myself at this point): "Look, Mr. T, it's getting late; sunset is practically over and I think you should be going" I tried to sound strong and in control, but God knew I really shaking inside.

"Shalis . . . I don't want to go. Please . . . Remember this . . ." and Mr. T went back down memory lane. He opened up and shared how disappointed he was that I didn't say anything at the time about his decision to get married and I had to tell him I didn't want to influence his decision to "do the right thing". It was not my place to do so, given he had (obviously) taken things to a new level with his then-girlfriend, now-wife. He replied that if he had known how I'd really felt, he would have changed his mind, but it was too late for "if only's" at this stage. Yes, our was a classic case of "too little, too late . . ."

I walked him to the door (which, thankfully when living in a flat, it's not too far away!). We stood there and he held me close . . . then tight, too tight; memory tight . . . and from somewhere, I let him go—I had to. I closed the door behind him and as the tears began to fall, my heart was crying out to God . . . when I heard "knock, knock" . . . Yes, I opened the door and yes, Mr. T was there. That night I broke my principles and he broke his vow in the flow of a bittersweet memory. When Mr. T eventually left, it was with mutual tears, recriminations and promises that we both knew we could never keep because I knew, in my heart and soul, I was NEVER, EVER going to see him again! Never!

Mr T. rang me a few days later and we agreed to meet up. I didn't want to see him but oh my God, I needed to hear his voice, I *needed* to see him, I needed *him*. We talked as we drove along about this and that, trying to skirt around and ignore the incident that had happened. (I knew I certainly wasn't going to bring it up, even though it was foremost in my mind.)

Journey Pause: *This was the proverbial elephant in the room no one wanted to mention! This situation was sitting up close and personal, right between us, on us and in us and there we were—play-arguing about the quickest route to get some place or other, what was the best Caribbean island and national dish. All tripe and trivia, when all the while, the elephant is slowly crushing and wearing us down . . . .*

Suddenly, in the midst of all the verbal roundabouts, he turned and asked me "did you mean it?"

"Eh? Mean what? What are you talking about?"

"What you said"

"Ermm, what *did* I say?" (I began to get scared, because I really could not remember!)

Mr. T started to laugh, "Shalisa, you mean you can't remember what you said!"

At this stage, I started to get annoyed because I was sure he was either playing games or trying to wind me up—and either way was not going to get a favourable response, trust me! "Shalisa! You mean, you don't remember telling me . . . you know . . . you know (at this stage, I was glaring at him!) you told me that you love me!"

I nearly crashed the car! "I told you what?!!" I could not believe my ears! You see, I had prided myself on being hard (ha-ha), tough (ha-ha) and, even though I might have thought it, felt it and wanted to say it, I never told anyone how I really felt. But he was right; at that time and in the moment, it seemed those words just came rushing out. (Didn't I tell you that what you bury in the dark will eventually come to light?) I was horrified but yet, relieved; he knew, I knew and the truth was out—at last. A couple of years late, admittedly, but I had finally been honest with myself, albeit at the wrong time and place.

Journey pause: It's amazing how often the truth shocks the one to whom it belongs. I was genuinely shocked to hear how I really felt from someone else. That experience taught me to be still and to listen to myself and to hear what I'm saying. Sometimes on our journey, we put up so many barriers that we have difficulty getting over them when the time comes. I now realize and recognize the need to do regular emotional self-checks, to ensure that where I am is where I want to be, and what I'm saying is the truth of what I have inside.

Sadly, I resumed my relationship with Mr. T and we continued for few more years, through many ups and downs. Finally, after much ducking and diving, internal angst and my feeling (and being) the proverbial hypocrite, he decided he and his wife were not suitable (apparently, his womanizing ways had finally caught up with him and she had had enough). So he was now free and we could, at last be together, right? Wrong! By then, I was with someone else and Mr. T now became *my* "contingency plan", *my* "back up", *my* "just-in-case", *my* "booty-call". Yep, having been played, I decided to become a "playa"! The only problem was, I wasn't sure how the game went, much less what the rules were! I decided *I* would call *him* if I had a need truly. Yes sistas, the "booty" was now on the other foot (okay, he wasn't to know that, but it sure made me feel gooood at the time!). Yes, it was now full on and for a short but intense period of time, it was great, exciting and wonderful—sex on tap! But if you don't have a good foundation or the right start, anything you then want or desire to build, cannot and will not stand.

Ours was not a healthy relationship and looking back at this point in my journey, I see us as limping along together in a badly organized 3-legged race where, although we might have started out in the same direction, life now found us trying to walk different paths. During that time, I began to seriously question my relationship with God and my behaviour as a "professed Christian". I felt I was not answerable or accountable to anyone, nor could anyone dare tell me anything different. For whilst in my social (church) circle, I was deemed the "goody-two-shoes", which was a persona I had been able to define and develop. In reality, I was much too scared to "leave" church and all that it stood for, in order to just be honest with myself about my lifestyle and desires.

Journey Pause*: Many of my church friends had left or were leaving to define themselves. Like a child that has to leave its home, so there comes a time in all of our lives, when we begin to question our value and belief systems; indeed, it's as if we need to go out to test them! But there are others like myself who, in wanting to go, are afraid; and we stay behind, hidden behind a curtain of other people's expectations, anticipations and perceptions, instead of testing that which we have been taught. This resulted in more secrecy, more hypocrisy, more hiding and covering up. Try to please everyone , we end up pleasing no one, least of all ourselves or our conscience.*

Payback

My time with Mr. T was slowly but surely (and thankfully) drawing to a close and the death knell was sounded when one day, he rang me out of the blue. As usual, when he had something unpleasant to say, the conversation would start with nervous laughter and jokes about the "good ol' times" and how much I meant to him (yeah, right!). Then Mr. T dropped another bombshell: he had gone to his GP (uh oh . . .) and had contracted an infection, a sexual "dis-ease" and I would need to go and get checked out . . . but "Honey, there's nothing to worry about!!"

My God! At a time when media attention was portraying Herpes and AIDS as silent but deadly killers, to get a call like that just made me think and expect the worst. I felt sick. I felt it was divine retribution for all my illicit relationships and double-dealings. I felt I was now, finally, at last, about to reap what I had sown and sown and sown. The chickens had indeed come home to roost and it was as if I could hear a faint echo " . . . yes, do NOT be deceived! Whatsoever a man sows, is what he will also reap". As Mr. T was talking, I was mentally preparing myself on how I could tell my family and friends I'd contracted the dreaded "H" or the big "A". I imagined being completely and utterly ostracized; I anticipated the tongue-wagging—and tongue lashings—from gossips and those just glad to see someone fall in shame and disgrace. I felt my life was well and truly over but, thank God, it wasn't as dire as I'd been imagining. It was a general sexual infection (if such a thing exists; because, by today's standards, it's practically considered a rite of passage amongst young people!)

I made an appointment to see my GP and was sent to "the clinic". It was there I believe God made sure I knew what I was there for and why. Every nurse, doctor, medical assistant was either African or Caribbean and their looks spoke volumes. During the pre-examination, a nurse asked me why I was there—and what I had. When I told her, she gave me a look which seemed to scream "Girl! You ought to know better!" The memory of lying on the examination table is forever imprinted on my mind. Lying there in an unfavourable position, I stared into the lights above my head trying to forget the probing, impersonal hands into secret places now being exposed. I had a lifetime on that table, as I had to face some hard, hard facts: what the hell was I doing in such a position? How and why did I allow it to happen?

Journey pause: So he looks good, smells good, walks, talks and loves good but take it from me, sista—all that glitters is definitely not always gold. My moments of hot passion and undying "lurve" ended with having to undergo a humiliating examination and a wake up call of a course of antibiotics. It could have been worse. I had to stop and question why I was actively participating in my own demise; why I was on a path of self-destruction via sexual immorality.

Okay, I could dress it up and cover it with bland sayings such as "But I love him!" "It's my body and I do what I want" "No one need ever know" "Well, what's good for the goose is good for the gander" . . . but the reality was a soul-embarrassing medical examination, having to deal with possible after effects of infertility and a life-time of suffering because I couldn't, wouldn't and didn't say "no". Was it worth it? Hell no! But did I go there again . . . Hmmm, stop and ask yourself that question because the sad fact is, most sistas get caught up in the moment (or just throw the moment away); we leave ourselves open to so much—not just sexually-transmitted infections and illnesses, but there's the emotional and relational dysfunction that we end up with and which sadly, for most of us, has become the norm—and for which medical science has yet to find a cure . . . .

After that experience, believe me when I say, my time with Mr. T had *definitely* come to an end. At last, I was able to see what my sister and friends were telling me about as I learned Mr-Look-Good ain't always good or right for me! Yep it was done, finally over . . . but don't you know that life has a way of just throwing a curve-ball? Some years later, I was at a function with my friends. A well-known South London "crew" was playing and guess who was there? Yes, Mr. T and yes, of course he made a huge show of meeting and greeting me (I think I forget to mention he was extrovert at best and down-right showy at worst!)

When one of my friends first saw him she was "Shalisa! Wow! Where you find this man? He's nice, blah, blah, blah!" I looked at AA and laughed and said "Hmmm, just wait and see!" During the evening, she kept trying to hook me up with him but by the end of the night, after being in close proximity to see, know and understand just what he was all about, she just kissed her teeth and said "Damn idiot! Shalisa, where you find him?!". Ha, I could have told her that!

Conclusion:

So, that's the end of my journey experience with Mr. T. I've chosen to share all these sordid details because I was speaking to a sista recently and sharing some elements of this experience with her. She had timidly opened up and shared a very personal moment of her own journey and I realized that hey, we go through life with so much baggage and think that we're the only one. We beat ourselves up because of past dysfunctional behaviour and even though it's not reflective of where we are now, we still relive the shame of yesteryear.

Journey Pause: *Sadly, this experience opened and prepared me for newer and more bittersweet memories of a similar nature. Because when you indulge in certain behaviours, you reinforce negative brain patterns and emotional responses. Painfully, I wasn't to realize the truth of that until some years later.*

My dear sista, you're not alone! You're not the only one to have messed up; the fact you're still in the land of living is a sign of hope; it's not all over! As you look back over your own life, I'm sure that you can see change—positive change—and growth. Don't let the past hold you back. Use each stumbling block as your stepping stone. Take this opportunity to open up those painful areas and apply the healing balm of self-forgiveness, understanding and love to yourself.

Sometimes we have acted in ways because of a root cause of ignorance, naivety, fear and even neediness. There are many deep-rooted issues which cause us to act in unfamiliar ways. When you're looking for love and acceptance, help and healing, strength and affirmation in all the wrong places, you will end up in similar situations. I share this brief journey experience (trust me, there is so much more!), because my primary aim is to **encourage** you.

I dare not judge anyone else's journey, and for those few times when I am tempted to point a disparaging finger at someone's journey faux pas, , my Mr. T experiences whisper softly but strongly from the corridors of time . . . "There but for the Grace of God . . . Go I". So be blessed and be encouraged . . . . you weren't the only one and you can still turn it around and go to where and what you have prayed, believed and hoped for.

CHAPTER 11

Pandora's Box.

Most of us have probably heard about Pandora's box. No? You haven't? Well, here's a synopsis for you:

> *In Greek mythology, Pandora was the first woman on earth. Zeus ordered Hephaestus, the god of craftsmanship, to create her and he did, using water and earth. The gods endowed her with many talents; Aphrodite gave her beauty, Apollo music, Hermes persuasion, and so forth. Hence her name: Pandora, "all-gifted".*
>
> *When Prometheus stole fire from heaven, Zeus took vengeance by presenting Pandora to Epimetheus, Prometheus' brother. With her, Pandora had a jar which she was not to open under any circumstance. Impelled by her natural curiosity, Pandora opened the jar, and all the evil contained (within) escaped and spread over the earth. She hastened to close the lid, but the whole contents of the jar had escaped, except for one thing which lay at the bottom, and that was Hope[2]*

Yes, that just about sums up what I'm about to share with you about this phase of my journey. Sometimes, when you think you have seen it all, done it all and tasted it all; when you believe you qualify for the t-shirt AND how to make it, something comes along to remind you that it's not all over yet! Life has yet another twist and turn. As has been said "what we think is the end of the road is just a bend in the road".

---

[2] "Pandora." *Encyclopedia Mythica* from Encyclopedia Mythica Online. <http://www.pantheon.org/articles/p/pandora.html> [Accessed July 01, 2009].

When you see something you have never seen before; when you hear something new or get a fleeting scent of a perfume which tantalises and entices you, that is what I am learning to call the beginnings or the findings of "Pandora's box".

Early in 2009, I fell in love. I mean, sticky-toffee apple love; sweet and smooth on the outside and crunchy, fresh and tart on the inside. It was a Pandora box-type of love just waiting for me to hold it and, as my curiosity grew, I could hold back no longer before tentatively sliding a fingernail inside and slowly, expectantly lifting the lid when—BAAM! It got me! All the while, when it was in the box, it was pure and perfect and sweet and divine and oh, just so very right; but once the lid had been lifted, wow! It was a vortex of emotions, a tsunami of feelings before it revealed itself for what it really was, emotional and almost psychological destruction. How and why did I open the box . . . ? Firstly, please take a seat as I invite you to accompany me as I revisit this part of my journey with you. Because when I start to remember, it is still very painful and very fresh in my mind and even now, my heart palpitates at the memory of it all.

I had been dating someone for three years and let me just pause here to tell you, that in itself was a miracle. I mean exclusive dating; no contingency plan, no Numbers 2, 3 or 4 stashed away "just in case" things did not work out; no "shadow man" waiting around the corner, no little black book, no midnight booty calls, nothing, nada. It was a very interesting time and experience to go through, as I thought we were "destined" to have a future together. But alas, the course of "true lurve" does not always run smooth and when he literally stood me up at the altar, so to speak, yet another chapter of love and life closed in my life regarding me and Mr X.

Journey Pause: *How many times do we rush in, not only where angels fear to tread, but also where fools would think twice about going? In desperation and loneliness, I allowed myself to be talked into a relationship with someone who looked the part but really was not my type at all. Honestly, there was nothing wrong with him, but how often have we sistas just "settled"; how many of us have carefully folded up a lifelong, even a childhood dream, put it away in a plastic vacuum* *and hidden it in the attic of our mind? How many of us have been, and indeed are still in relationships, where we've chosen to bury ourselves, our real selves, in order to be seen as having the trappings of a "normal relationship"? Yet we are still unable to silence that voice, yes, you know the one I mean, our inner voice which is always screaming for recognition and release. How many of us have felt trapped by external circumstances, opinions and expectations and instead of living, we end up living live in mediocrity, following the same pattern day in and day out? Like I keep saying: sista, trust me, you are not alone!*

Looking back, I believe I was going through a relationship grieving process. I grieved the time spent in trying to make something happen which obviously had a time limit and a "please use by" date on it. I mourned the covenant privileges shared with someone who had little or no desire to enter into a commitment or covenant of any sort with me. I relived broken promises and shattered dreams and had to hear the echo of my own questions reverberate in my mind only to get the same answers in return. I therefore decided to take matters into my own hands; I'd had enough of being a victim, it was time to be a victor! Previously, I did my own thing and I decided I'd had enough of listening to the dreams, wishes, hopes and desires of others, who maybe wanted to exercise and/ or practise their prophetic utterances on me. No, I figured I could do bad all by myself—so why allow anyone else to do it to me? I would take matters into my own hands to make it happen so see if I could find someone for me, someone who was attracted to me and was "my type". Warning: when you're love-starved with only a myriad of dysfunctional relationships as your only example, taking such a stance is a disaster just waiting to happen.

So I decided to "get with it" and join an internet dating agency. Listen: the media adverts were practically telling me the only way to find my ideal, supa-dupa love and life partner was to join up and get matched up—which I did! A proverbial Pandora's Box was before me, looking so inviting and enticing; surely, what could go wrong! I was relatively streetwise (after a fashion) and felt internet dating would give me a sense of control as to who *I* wanted. It was man-shopping online; you see it, view it, click it and hey presto, your desired package arrives in a few days! However, with hindsight, I guess deep down in my inner self, I simply wanted someone—anyone—to see me, like me or even to notice me. Yes, I wanted the chocolate box and rose-covered cottage experience of someone desiring and even needing me for a change, because how my previous relationship had ended, I was in need of a huge pick me up.

Yes, Pandora's box was just asking to be opened and everything was in place and set for its release. I made the momentous decision to break up with Mr X and the resultant grieving process was made all the worse because it was in the public domain. Others who knew about "us" would often ask me for him and what was happening, usually at those times when I felt I was getting over everything. Like many other women who make a decision to follow their conscience and not the dictates of others, such a move is usually questioned. I was asked the following, in various ways and from many people, 'Why, if you are looking for a significant other, give up on and move away from someone who, to all intents and purposes, is husband-material?" Believe me it was not an easy decision but one which I knew I had to make. Further more, I had a premonition via a couple of dreams which alerted me to the fact that where I was going, he was not willing or prepared to go.

Journey Pause: *Sometimes, we allow the following to keep and hold us in toxic situations, places and relationships, which for our own sanity, we need to move away from. It's what I call the **L.F.D.P Syndrome**. This is where "Loneliness, Frustration, Desperation &/or Persuasion", either singularly or together, are motivating factors as to why we stay in situations, places, circumstances and with people which, if we're honest enough to admit to ourselves—or were even having to advise a sista-girlfriend about it—we would be the first to champion the need for the person to leave, move on and out, whilst encouraging them that yes, you CAN do better. Not that the person they're with is essentially a **bad** person, but rather the person (or situation, etc) just isn't right for your friend. Now, if we can and would do that for a sista-friend, why oh why, can't, won't and don't we do that for ourselves? When either one or all of those factors—loneliness, frustration, desperation or persuasion—sets in or attacks, there's a tendency to react, usually in negative and non-productive way, where we emotionally "self-harm". As a seemingly "I've-got-it-all-together" woman, none of us want to be perceived as having anything wrong, especially in this area. So we* *ignore the warning signs within and without. We are not proactive but it's only when things go wrong that we are forced to try to do some damage control . . . often at a serious cost and sadly, when it can be too late . . . .*

After a while, I began to pick my self up. I threw myself into ministry work, exercise and staying at the office after hours, in the hope of numbing the pain. The resultant countless late nights meant I was too tired to think or feel when I finally collapsed in bed. One night, I was watching a gospel channel and saw an advert for a Christian internet dating site and thought "Why not!" I saw it as a chance to find my own man, to forge my own path and to pick my own special someone to taste! I remember praying before I logged on and filled in the relevant information. I was on my way! I was so excited and saw it as my way of telling the world at large that I was capable and regaining some control of my life; for surely, doesn't God help those who help themselves?

So I tentatively logged on, joined up and began my search. I was like a kid in a candy store! So many options and selections from chocolate brown, rich espresso to café au lait and vanilla ice were all there for the asking! Young, old, black, white—and all non-fattening too! With glazed eyes and a hungry heart, I strolled up and down the aisles of this cyber-candy store and boy, did it feel good!

Like Pandora, my fingers just could not resist touching the box, stroking the box, holding the box and turning it around and over, just watching the light reflect and bounce on it. It was a wonderful experience to imagine each prospective "suitor" could be "the one". But after a while, I got bored. How come, I hear you ask? Because my search for my ideal man, my life and soul partner was taking too long. It was not just about age and a ticking body clock; it was about wanting what I felt was my due; it was time, *my* time, to have *my* life and to begin to enjoy it. However, it was not as successful as I had thought and becoming somewhat discouraged, I abandoned my search for a few weeks or so.

Until that eventful day it all changed, when I received a long awaited message in my personal inbox "you've got mail!". Well, you can imagine the grin on my face; I was back—and this time, someone had seen me!

There's something that just lights up when you get a message saying someone has seen *you* and wants to contact *you* with a view to getting to know *you*. I found it very comforting and empowering. So with beating heart, I logged on (why my heart was beating faster than normal considering I was not actually meeting the person makes me laugh when I look back; I guess it was the sense of anticipation and expectation).

I tentatively opened the email, rather like a child opening a first Christmas present, and saw . . . HIM. Tall, dark curly hair with sun kissed skin and an inviting moustache; he was just what the doctor ordered to end my relationship malaise. But it was his accompanying message, which went straight to my heart. As he was not, dare I say, one of my usual "chocolate box" favourites, I felt maybe, just maybe, God was trying to tell me something. In hindsight, I recognise He was probably shouting "NO, NO! Put it back!", but hey, Pandora's box was just too irresistible, believe me, and so I started my first on line dating relationship. I felt in control (ahha, the "c" word again!); I felt empowered, excited and alive for the first time in a long, long time.

After several heartfelt, open and sensitive emails, I sensed a shift in my heart. I really, really wanted this to work; I saw it as the panacea for all my problems, the proverbial "quick fix". I allowed myself to believe what he was saying because it had been too long since anyone had ever spoken to me like that. I mean, he knew what to say, how to say, when to say and even *where* to say it. You see, he "touched" me in secret places with his words and unearthed hidden and long forgotten dreams and desires. I allowed myself to open up and trust because I *wanted* to believe, I *wanted* to open up and trust again, for I had been closed and shut down for so long

Journey Pause*: For anyone out there who has ever wondered how to start loving and exercising their faith—that is a lesson right there . . . When we have allowed life to knock us down and to keep us down, in whatever area and arena the bout took place, we forget that we, yes you and I, ultimately have the final choice as to whether we stay down or, with muscles straining and body paining, we make one final, strenuous effort to refocus and get back up again. In making—a decision to love again, to at least* want *to love again, was the first step towards being free . . . and to becoming "me" again . . . .*

His emails filled me. They fed me and I ate them. I was hungry and he was giving me the food my soul craved for—and he used the ingredients which appealed to me—words. Being very spiritual, his messages reached straight to the core of me that is seldom ever touched by a man. His poignant expressions about his love and desire for God brought tears to my eyes. When he shared his dreams, his hurts, his disappointments, I wanted to just hold and comfort him . . . . and when he shared his desires and intentions for and with me, they made me smile, dream . . . and smile again. As my online "relationship" progressed, I *knew* he was "the one". I knew we were going to get married. I was going to move to America or even Australia (although the last option should have given me a *serious* clue). Reading through rose-coloured glasses, I rationalised the sale of my house, moving to where my love would take me and that Mum would be taken care of because doesn't God always take care of His own? Yes sistas, I had it all sorted and worked out in my mind.

Journey Pause: *Needy is defined as being "in need of practical or emotional support; distressed." Hmm, a lot of women don't like to admit this, so I will say it on their—and your—behalf. I was needy and when you're needy, you are open to any and everything. What do I mean? A baby will eat and suck anything because that is an automatic response inherently programmed within them so they can meet their needs. Indeed, anything a baby or toddler grabs hold of usually goes into their mouth, because, at that age and stage of life, it's their only point of reference. (Why am I sharing this with you, this deeply personal and somewhat embarrassing experience? Because having fallen, I want to warn people, especially my sistas, of the pitfalls that await you when you think you're of a certain age, creed or colour and that life and love is passing you by. I don't want L.F.P.D or neediness to divert or distract you on your own journey experience . . .)*

I have to be honest and confess that touching and opening Pandora's box, at least in the first stage, felt so good, exciting and emotionally electrifying! It was invigorating and let's not forget, downright thrilling! How many of you know that, when a woman is in "lurve", things began to look right and fit tight?! I resumed my exercise regime and dusted off the cross trainer which, up until then, was being used as a clothes rack when ironing clothes! I began to eat right and monitor my health. Indeed, my outlook and demeanour changed for the better and even my sister recognised there was a glow about me and a pep in my step. Do bear in mind all of this was not intentional, it was a natural reaction to being loved (or at least, having the perception of being loved) by someone else. Being in this place and in this heightened state of emotion, just made me feel more alive and the fact it was a secret, *my* secret, made it extra special.

So, with my hands poised to go to my next level in life, I was ready to lift the lid on Pandora's box . . . I was in love! I loved this man and the enormity, the strength and depth of those feelings completely overwhelmed me. My prayers, my smiles, my tears, my *everything* was for and about this man, someone I had never met but who filled my waking moments. When he mentioned "marriage", "wife" "you and me" in the same email, I nearly passed out! We began to talk about a future together—our future and getting married. I was over 100% sure that he was from God, for does God not order my steps; is He not interested in my life? Surely He had sent this Adam, this "Boaz" to rescue me from mid-life mediocrity, a life of shame and reproach; he had come to take me away from pitying glances and (imagined) stifled laughs about my relationship status . . . especially the last one. Like I said . . . I was needy . . .

Journey pause*: Let me take a few moments on my journey to share this with you: when you date and break up and only a few people know, it's hard but you get over it. However, when it is a community affair and too many people know all about it, you find you have to keep on explaining and smiling and repeating over and over as to why the person is no longer with you (even though you really don't know)—and it is hard, very, very hard. It is humiliating and painful and you just want to find a safe haven, somewhere to run and hide, preferably in the arms of someone,* anyone *else.*

So we continued our correspondence. He phoned me and we talked and our "relationship" grew and like seeds planted in moist, fertile soil, it was regularly watered with sweet words and heartfelt longings. I'd put my hand on Pandora's box and oh, so slowly, began to ease it open. I anticipated the ending without having had the reality of a beginning (or even knowing what it was). I know this might sound crazy for a mature and educated woman, but I had tasted him; not sexually or even physically, but in my mind, body and soul, I *felt* him; I *knew* him. I had willingly opened myself to him and let him into the inner, the real me. It was not infatuation or desire, it wasn't even "lurve" but I was in love. I loved MC, the image I had unwittingly and so desperately conjured up of him. This was one script I knew the ending of; I knew how this love affair was going to play out. Ours was going to be the matrimonial wonder of the 21st century.

I began to allow myself to imagine the joy, real lasting joy, of having found my soul mate and know that, he truly was "the one" (yep, sounds just like a line from the Matrix!) I saw us loving, laughing and living and even having disputed "fall outs"—just so we could have fun making up again, again . . . and again. This was the "will of God" and we were in it; I knew it, I *felt* it. Yet, as Pandora's Box slowly opened, what I'd imagined to be a sweet melody emanating from its velvety darkness was in reality a discord from where nightmares originate. For it was in opening what I thought was a dream at last come true, that MC dropped the bombshell.

Inauguration

I'd previously booked a passage to witness history in the making—the inauguration of the first Afro-American President of the United States of America! I knew I had to be there—it couldn't happen without me! I was due to leave London on Friday 17th January 2009 and remember the series of events only too well. I had everything set up and was ready for Obama's inauguration but was to painfully discover that I too, would be taken a step higher to a place I'd never imagined. When I had shared my plans with MC, you know he suggested we meet up! At last, the shadow was about to become substance and trust me, I almost didn't need to book a ticket as I was practically airborne on wings of "lurve!"

On Monday, my e-lover rang me eager and excited because at last, we were going to see each other in a few days time. His words aroused and awakened me; I now understood the meaning of "telephone sex" (told you this was raw!). Being wordy, he really knew how to swing a simile, announce an adjective, nail a noun and verify a verb, for real . . . umm humm! I no longer walked, I floated; never, ever in my life had I experienced that and I have had plenty of experiences in the past.

Journey pause: In remembering this painful part of my journey and share this experience, please note the use of humour is not to trivialise but to help anaesthetise the pain, so forgive me; I am not being deliberately trite or frivolous

I knew that my life was going to change from 17th January onwards. On Tuesday he told me he was "leaving home" (ha!) to come to London, England via France. I could hardly wait or contain myself! Emails were out the window now, it was phone calls, voice-to-voice interaction and boy, that was sweeter still. Having fallen hook, line and sinker for this man, I was completely besotted by "him". He rang Wednesday morning to say he was on his way and would see me in London the following day. (Yep, I'm sure you know what is coming . . .) But on Thursday morning, I got the call that was to change my life and my opinion of myself. Have you ever done something that shocks even you? You stop look in a mirror wondering who that strange person is stranger staring back at you, and you wonder where and when the *real* you had gone . . . Well, that was me on that memorable Thursday morning.

I remember it well. I was running late for work and it was a grey, overcast, dull day, the type that only encourages you to into wanting to go on holiday with a lover you've never met and to spend your life with a man that may not exist . . . MC had rung me earlier that morning to say he'd been detained by the French immigration authorities and was now not allowed to proceed further and yes folks, that's when the drama took a new turn and "MC" really came into his own. He was a master player because he played me like a one-woman orchestra. He cried, he begged, he implored. He strummed my heart strings like a Stradarvis violin. I can acutely remember the ache in the pit of my stomach; something was wrong; this was not supposed to happen, this was *not* supposed to happen! I tried to snatch back and hold onto the dream which was fast becoming a nightmare from the brink of my reality but, no, he rang again.

"Shalisa, honey, baby; I need some money! Babes, only you can help me! Please, please! You know I love you and I wouldn't ask you, but I don't have anyone else. Please babes . . . You can ring Pastor M to verify what I'm saying because he's trying to raise some of the cash needed for me to get outta here to see you. Babes, I can't stand it! To come this far and not see you, babes, don't let me stay here".

Journey Pause: *Now, for those sistas with sense and who are in their right minds, I know you'd already seen this coming, right at the beginning of the chapter. Yet, hold on a minute: there is another person, another sista, who is silently crying because she recognises that, unbelievably, she is not alone in having been unceremoniously duped and conned; she's not alone in having given her heart and emotions before checking out the facts. She realises someone else has experienced the heartache and pain, the humiliation and shame of loving a stranger from afar and too soon. The papers are filled with numerous women who, in their quest for love and acceptance, willingly believe the unbelievable in order to gain what never really existed and so give themselves before they've given their material goods, to men promising that rarest of commodities—love. I too used to laugh at such stories and ridicule the mental and emotional state of such "foolish" women, until I found myself living their story . . .*

I remember getting off the bus outside my local bank. It was raining; maybe it was angels crying at what was to come. I remember calling him back (!) to tell him I wasn't sure of this; I didn't think I could do it; I had no money of my own, for by that time, I was desperate to get out of the pit that I was fast descending in. Ohh, but if *you* had heard him, believe me, you might well have had a hard time saying no as well, because he was good, really good. I mean, no Hollywood actor could have matched him in this role and, coupled with the fact, the hard cold fact, I was "in love", only just exacerbated the situation and how I was feeling. My emotions were strung like a high wire over the Niagara Falls and I was too far gone to turn back now; the only choice was to inch my way across.

I looked across the road and saw a Western Union outlet but no, I couldn't . . . could I? I remember all reason, sense and rationale seeming to drain from me as zombie-like, I walked into the Bank and withdrew over two grand, yes, *two thousand pounds* from my mother's account. Yes, you read correctly. I stole from my Mum, my *Mother*, for a "man" I had never met or even seen. I was cold outside and numb inside; yes, the weather just mirrored how I felt—grey, miserable . . . and dead. MC had told me that he would repay the money on his arrival and even sent me photos of a large cache of US dollars that he had on him but by then, that was no longer the issue. For the first time in my life, I had stolen; I mean really stolen from someone I love, from someone, the only one, who ever really loved and cared for me—and still does. Tears? What are tears? Don't you know you can reach a point of such shame and self loathing where tears refuse to come, as if they themselves want no part in what you have done? I was past crying. I remember putting that huge wad of money in my bag and like a programmed assassin I rang back for my next set of instructions.

Journey Pause: *Now, even as I relieve this experience, I have to stop and ask myself what the hell happened?!! What was going on? How? Why? To even "ring back for my next set of instructions" is, I believe, an apt description. I can now understand, to a small degree, what it is to be abused and to still want to be intimate with the abuser. I might have scoffed at never having been beaten but by then, I had taken some serious blows to my self-esteem, my integrity and my conscience.*

I was unable to conduct the requested money transfer from my local Western Union (like I said, God was *really* trying to tell me something!) and instead opted to use one nearer to where I worked, in South London. (Why am I naming places and specific areas? Because it was real; *I* did it and although sharing it is a painful experience, it's also a necessary cathartic exercise and part of the healing.) I remember walking like a programmed zombie to the Western Union, where I rang the so-called Pastor M for instructions; boy, was I ever obedient—which is what being conned and emotionally abused will do for and to you.

Journey Pause: *This event was a strategic and well planned set up. "Pastor M" was a part of the elaborate con spun by MC and his cohorts. It seems that such people access certain websites to then be able to prey on the vulnerable, needy . . . and downright foolish. Listen, I've just to*

be real and tell it as it is—or at least how it was for me. "Pastor M"
actively encouraged me to listen to MC who, he claimed, was a true man
of God, someone who loved the Lord. May God have mercy on those
charlatans and crooks that misuse and abuse the name and character of
God for their own ends by feeding on needy, lonely, vulnerable women
who are their victims.

I rang MC to let him know the price of my love had been paid because, can you really put a price on love, true love, soul-mate kind of love? Ha, but the dam began to break because you can only kid yourself for so long. For up until that point, I thought I was so strong. Even though I'd (finally) confided in my sister about him, and despite her loving counsel and prayers for "God's will to be revealed and the truth to be known", guess what, I was NOT ready nor prepared to listen and, truth to be told, I was hell bent on making it work . . . .

I continued my journey to work, with a growing, nauseous feeling in my stomach and my emotions were no better. As previously mentioned, even Mother Nature was letting me know all was not well, as being unusually grey and miserable day, even the rainfall seemed lethargic and spiritless. I arrived late at work and, would you believe, had the cheek to go out again and take out *another* amount from my Mum's account—this time *over* two thousand pounds. I now realise the truth of the saying that when you do something once, it becomes easier the second time. It was like the catchphrase from University Challenge: I had started and so I will finish. I was on a mission and rationalised that hey, once MC and I met, of course he'd repay me the money (because he had *promised*, right! Ha-ha!) and Mum wouldn't even have to know anything was missing. Why, she'd probably laugh at my cheeky bravado and daring when she saw how happy I was with my "love". Oh yes, at long, long, *long* last, I had effectively kicked my conscience to the kerb and was sole controller of my life, my life; I was mistress of my own destiny. I was woman ~ watch me roar, but little did I know it would turn into a broken whimper . . .

Journey pause: *Doesn't this make you want to puke?! Yet that was where I was . . . and no, it's not pretty, it's not sweet and it sure as hell ain't nice. For those who know me, I mean, really* know *me, when I'd finally* *plucked up the courage (and shame) to tell them this, their collective reaction was "Shalisa, you sure? What happened? That's not like you!?! What got into you?!? Now, when you're faced with a question like that, what answer can you give? I was only able to tell my best friend some 3-4 months after it happened because I was so ashamed and sure that she would kick me to the kerb, spit on me and walk away. Honestly, that's how I felt and imagined she'd react to me. Yet I'm sharing this because somewhere, out there, is a woman, a sista, on her own journey, who is having to deal with the ghosts of her past . . . and possibly her future. I am here to tell you . . . it ain't over; it just ain't over! The fact that you are here, reading this . . . take it from me . . . it ain't over. No matter what, where, how, when, why you did what you did and done what you done, believe me, your journey ain't ended.*

It didn't stop there. Mr. MC rang me on Thursday night to say, through crocodile tears, demands, cajoling and emotional bullying, that the money wasn't enough and I would have to send more. CLANG! That is when the penny finally dropped. Like Pandora who opened the box expecting to find gold, jewels and treasure beyond her wildest imagination, the façade I'd so willingly and foolishly built up in the castles of my mind, was exposed for what it was. It all came rushing out, sadness, poverty and death, because on that day, something in me died. Like the moths that attacked and stung Pandora when she opened the box and brought sickness, dis-ease and death into the world, I thought my life would never be the same again—and I was right. I was ready to give up, give in and throw away the towel, because, how and who could I teach and encourage to live right and walk well . . . but wait . . . shhh, what's that noise . . . ?

Journey pause: In the immediate aftermath, as I lay in the foetal position on my bed, with each heart beat sounding out the death knell in my mind, I began to hear a different sound, silently, ohh, so silently . . . shhh, if you listen, really be still and listen, you can hear it . . .

"All that was left in the box was Hope. It fluttered from the box like a beautiful dragonfly, healing Pandora's wounds. Pandora may have let pain and sadness into the world but she also let Hope out to follow

them"[3] *However, at the time, I was not able to recognise or perceive any possible good coming out of this but I thank God I was still long enough to listen . . .*

The Night before the Day After

As stated, I was due to fly out to the States on Friday 17th January but I couldn't go. Thursday night found me in a state of shock, as the realisation, the enormity of what I had actually done, started to hit home . . . and to hit me. I don't know how I got through that day at work or even how I reached home but when I got in, racked with guilt and conscience-stricken, I avoided Mum like the plague and went straight to my room, curled up on the bed a foetal position and just lay there, racking my now defogged brain on how to get myself out of this s . . . t (why is it that you always seem to get instant clarity *after* the fact—and never before?*)*

In desperation and a foolish attempt to try to salvage something, *anything*, I decided to go back to the source. I managed to find and log onto my PC in an attempt to contact him but that was too slow, so I rang Mr. MC. I could not believe what I was hearing! I don't know how long he was prepared to keep spinning this yarn, rather like a spider who still keeps throwing out more silk, even though the fly's been caught; she just can't help it. He was asking for yet *more* money from the proverbial cash cow! It was then, the cold, dark, dank feeling that I was to carry around for the next few months came to stay: it was then I realised I had been scammed; not just money (my *Mum's* money), but my feelings, my emotions, my heart. I could not believe that I, Shalisa, had been scammed! That I, Shalisa, had stolen from my Mum—for a man! That I, Shalisa, had allowed myself to be such a blasted idiot and that I, Shalisa, I was still in England when I should have been on a plane on the way to New York! I did what any woman would do—I put my face in the pillow and SCREAMED . . . .

---

[3]   Source: http://myths.e2bn.org/mythsandlegends/playstorysen562-pandoras-box.html

Do you know that when you get a cut or a gash that, after the initial searing pain has passed, the white blood cells then rush to ground zero to begin the healing process? This is the body's way of reminding us that we can't stay down forever! We have to get up one day . . . someday and often, the healing process usually starts with a friend. On that eventful Friday afternoon, AA rang to see how Mum was doing . . . and was shocked to hear *me* answer the phone! In between tears, all I could tell her was "AA, I can't talk right now; something's happened . . . no, no, it's not Mum; she's alright (I nearly puked when I said that, because I knew different, even though I'd not told her at the time). AA, I'll call you later. Just pray for me, please, okay. Bye". How could I tell my best friend what I'd done?

You know, whenever I've read or heard someone say that time stood still, I just dismissed it as a load of poppycock but there was no poppy or cock that day: it really did seem to freeze. Everything seemed to stay the same with only me moving in and out of each painful timeframe. Now this is where it gets kinda crazy-er! As I was lying on the bed, having to deal with my own self-inflicted wounds, wondering how the hell I was going to get out of this mess, how I could ever tell Mum much less repay her, I had a couple of visitors. Not flesh and bones, but I "saw" them; they were real.

I remember the starkness with which they appeared and presented their solutions, their way out. One said "Suicide. I'm your only way out. Just kill yourself. If you want to repay your Mum and give her back her hard-earned money, just kill yourself. You've got insurance; they'll pay up and it'll all be settled in one easy go", but the thought of suicide only exacerbated my guilt-ridden feelings. I realised not only would Mum know I was a thief, but she'd have to find even more money to bury me as remember, I had severely depleted her life savings.

No, the other "visitor" was more practical and pragmatic because it suggested using something I'd used before, although never to such depths. "Prostitution. You can do it. Just go to a different part of town; even make a day trip of it, a couple times a month and I'm sure you'll get the money back in no time. This way, you live and can repay. Yes honey, just use the thing Mama done gave you!"

Now, you may or may not believe me, but their suggestions hit me hard—BOOM. Listen, I'm telling it as it is—their hellish suggestions impacted me and shook me to my core because I was ready to do something, *anything*, to try to make amends, reverse and change back all that had gone before. It was real and the suggestions were real . . . but I thank God, I really thank God, for the little whisper left in Pandora's box . . . Hope.

I thought of ringing DeeDee and faced, what was yet, another battle. Remember my two "visitors"? They did not want me to ring. Now, this is really going to sound like I'm off the Richter scale, but there was a literal battle in my mind. Prostitution was winning hands down, but it was only when I thought of men of different nationalities, colours and creeds touching and *entering* me, that Hope's voice began to get louder . . . I decided to ring DeeDee and picked up the phone, only to put it down again and kept repeating this pattern for over an hour. After a determined effort, I remember in desperation shouting out: "I'm going to tell DeeDee!" and resigning myself to being ostracised by my lil' sista. Was it truly all this dramatic? It was all that and more, because it was pitiful and true. When I spoke to DeeDee, I remember crying and telling her something bad, really bad, had happened and that I wasn't able to go to America. I didn't have any money (talk about irony or what!) and basically, I didn't know what to do.

Now DeeDee, knows how to deal with me when I'm having or going through a crisis; she keeps quiet and listens. Well, this was no exception. After a little while, when my tears had stopped and she was able to make sense of my garbled message, she quietly said "Shalis, I have to ask you: did you meet someone else? Have you slept with someone else?" My response was "No, but I'd rather have slept with the Household Cavalry than this!" Believe me when I say DeeDee was now truly worried!

It seemed to take ages and ages for me to tell her what had happened, in each painful detail, leaving nothing out . . . and there it was—silence. The silence I knew would come and which I'd dreaded, a silence which seemed to speak volumes. The silence that confirmed my worthlessness, the silence which kept growing and growing and growing, threatening to cut me off from family and friends and life itself . . . when I suddenly heard: "Shalis, let's pray"—and DeeDee began to minister to me. I can't remember what she said that night, because it wasn't my ears that she spoke into, it was my spirit.

Journey Pause: *Trust me, this is not about "religion" or hocus-pocus, but there are times when someone's words will by-pass the natural ear to resonate within our very being. This was just one of those moments. Hope came alive; a faint fluttering, an irregular heart-beat . . . but it was alive, nonetheless, it was alive.*

I thanked her and tearfully asked if she and her husband would please, please, *please* come down as I knew I HAD to tell Mum that night. I realised and had determined that, whatever happened, this thing, this situation, which seemed to have a stronghold on me, wasn't gonna keep me in it's grip for any longer. I was prepared to face the music and in the words of Susan Jeffers, to "feel the fear and do it anyway". Now, all this time, I'd been in my room, only coming out for essentials, like the bathroom and kitchen and so, every time I saw Mum, I'd just grunt and pass by, as if *she* had done *me* something.

It knows it was my guilt which made me unable to talk, and sistas, I know you feel me!. I managed to grunt out to Mum (trust me, I could hardly look at her, much less talk) that DeeDee and her husband were coming to see *us* that evening. Mum, with her pragmatic and phlegmatic self, just took it in her stride and said okay. She never asked me a thing.

Suddenly, it came. Despite another family appointment, my sister and brother-in-law managed to juggle and change it round. We all knew this was a real-life, family emergency.

I clearly remember what happened next. When they knocked the door, I called Mum and she went and sat in the front room, in her armchair. When I opened the door, my brother-in-law just hugged me and said "It's going to be alright, it's going to be alright; don't worry, it's going to be alright". Those words are etched in my mind forever. I expected condemnation, a barrage of recriminations and downright disgust—but instead, I received comfort from a much unexpected source.

DeeDee and her husband came in. The four of us were in the sitting room but it felt so crowded and stifling. After some perfunctory greetings, DeeDee said "Aunty Monica, I'd like to pray. We need to ask God for His healing, His mercy and above all, His grace and forgiveness". Mum just sat there, like she was ready and expecting a bullet in the head. After DeeDee prayed, I took a deep breath and just plunged in and told Mum the whole sorry story. No embellishments, no excuses, no "I-don't-know-what-happened". I just "fessed up and told it as it was. Now, that is the essence of me; I've always prided myself that if I am wrong, if I was big and bad enough to *do* it, I've got to be big and bad enough to *confess* it. I told Mum *everything* about Mr. MC, the internet dating, the phone calls . . . and the money. After I'd finished, it seemed as if every word just hung in the air; you could literally see all what I'd just said hanging there, suspended just below the lights, like a cloud, just waiting, waiting, waiting.

Then it came: Mum gave a deep sigh and said "Well, I guess there are lessons to be learned from this. Yes, there are lessons to be learned. How much money was taken? Okay, well that money could've helped you pay off some of your debts (*now THAT is another story!)* Okay, well, it could've been worse"—and that was it. I sat there in shock; even DeeDee looked surprised, because she later confided in me "Shalisa, your mum is a strong woman, a lot stronger than I thought! I thought she'd have had a heart attack or say something, but she didn't say a negative word to you about it. Shalis, you see God! He *knew* this was going to happen and although He could have stopped it, it was *allowed* it happen for a reason".

Well! I sat there and I distinctly remember thinking (or hearing . . .) "This is what grace and forgiveness is; I am experiencing true forgiveness, grace and love". Often in religious circles or at sentimental moments, we talk about grace, mercy and forgiveness without ever having fully experienced the giving or receiving of it. Well, that night, I got it—I really did. I understood those terms as never before.

Journey Pause: *No, there was no gold at the bottom of the rainbow; in fact, there was NO rainbow! No choral music sang, no angelic beings,* *no bright lights but the hope that was in Pandora's Box was beginning to take root. Never in my life can I remember the tangibility of forgiveness, grace and love as at that moment. It kept me from sinking and staying in a pit of self-destructive thinking and behaviour. It gave me hope to believe again and in the days, weeks and months following, it helped to maintain me. I began to allow God and life to begin healing and remaking me, a process I called "taking baby steps".*

Fast forward to May 2009 to the launch of a women's conference I was planning and facilitating, titled "From Gutter to Glory".

Journey Pause: *Believe it or not, in the midst of all of this, I was still ministering and attending church; still standing and praying (and crying as often as not!) every week. Still planning and preparing and attending the regular women's meetings, all in the aftermath of what had happened. I was still daring to tentatively come to God in my "quiet times" where I'd sit and dare not say anything because I did not know what to say. I was still doing but scarcely feeling.*

To all those sistas who know and love God but who have "fallen", whether in sexual sin, financial misappropriation, even if you've been caught gossiping—whatever the sin, whatever the situation, please know God has not forgotten you nor has He kicked you to the kerb. There were many texts that strengthened and kept me at that time, the sweetest one being ". . . for God so loved the world that He gave His only Son". God loved me enough to send His Son to die for me and I began to know, I mean, really know, that He loved and loves me still . . . and He's willing to work with and in me.

At the Conference we witnessed a powerful move of God, as many women were delivered and encouraged to recognise and accept the love of a God Who is willing and able to take you from the gutter of your past, the gutter of your circumstances, the gutter of your situations and walk with you, to the glory of your destiny and future, into a glory He has ordained for you.

Journey Pause: *Dear Reader! It is NOT all over! God is able to do more than you could ever know, believe or imagine! So you had an abortion? God can move you from your gutter to glory! You've been in prison for this, that or the other—only you know your crime and your circumstances!—God is willing to set you free from the gutter of your past to the glory of your future! You've lost faith, you've never really understood or you simply have never really believed in God—why not give God a chance to move you from the gutter of painful doubt and wistful longing to a glory of a real relationship with Him?*

Sex, drugs, abusive or abusing behaviour—whatever the spectrum of despair which landed you in the gutter of life in the first place, know this fact: there IS hope for you! Yes, even if you've tried covering it up with the latest make up and accessories, we all know no amount of brand names or designer clothing can hide your longing to be somewhere and, dare I say it, someone, different. Why not give God a chance and let Him give you something glorious and beyond your wildest dreams . . .

After the last night at the conference, DeeDee took me to one side and said "Shalis, *this* is what the enemy was trying to keep you from regarding that situation with Mr MC! You see what God has started! Shalisa, just wait and see if God doesn't turn things around for you".

Tribute? Who, Me?

January 2010: I was privileged to be honoured with a love offering by the women's group at my church. It was a complete and utter surprise because they didn't know, how could they know, what I'd been through the past year? When the announcement was made and I was called up, I cried, I cried;. Actually, it is what is my Jamaican sistas would call "cow bawling!" I stood there and just had to cover my face and weep. I wept to know the reality of God's mercy, His love, His forgiveness, His grace, His compassion; I wept because of a new start, a fresh beginning; I wept because of my own unworthiness; I wept because of sins forgotten, forgiven and covered and of a new life restored. Yes, I wept because God had truly taken me out of the gutter of my own making to begin to (finally) walk into His glory.

Journey Pause:

Dear sista . . . don't turn this page over and think it's impossible; don't think it's a fairy tale or just "religious ramblings". This chapter took me so long to complete, because it was very difficult to go back and uncover and remember. At times, I really didn't think it'd be possible for me to finish this, but here it is; my personal testimony to love, grace (undeserved mercy) and favour. My journey is still unfolding and taking shape because of the One Who has walked and continues to walk with me. Won't you allow Him to walk with you through your dark places? Won't you allow Him to touch and heal your wounded spirit and soul? Won't you just confess all that you are and are not to Him and allow Him to cover you, to hold you, to comfort and to love you . . . ? He's right there, waiting for you to say "Come Lord, come". He is the One Who is ever near", for He is the One who has walked with you in all your darkest, scariest and loneliest moments and His hand is still reaching out in love to you. The fact you are still here means you've still got a destiny to reach—Pandora's Box may have been a disaster but there is still Hope . . . Just be still and listen for it . . .

CHAPTER 12

Time to Get Back Up Again

Finale

So my experiences of "She Who Walks Alone . . . with One" have come to an end, at least for this, the first stage of my journey. Writing this has been a healing experience, enabling me to go back, way back in time and revisit long-forgotten places and faces. I've been able to remember, to feel, to live and relive . . . and to finally give God thanks for having brought me this far.

My journey is still in progress. I'm still going through and even with so much knowledge behind me; I recognize I am in desperate need for true wisdom to learn how to apply it for where I am now. Yes, it's been a lonely path. Not because I didn't have friends or anyone to share it with; far from it! If it wasn't for friends and family (especially my sister), I know I wouldn't have made it to where and who I am today. Yet, it's been lonely in that each experience, each moment, each footstep is one only I could have. I had to go through things for myself, in order to know the truth I now know.

When my sister and I used to talk and I began to open up and share with her some of my relational experiences, she'd often say "Shalis, one day God is going to use your experiences to help other women! You will tell them what you've been through and they'll know that there is hope." Now DD wasn't being disparaging or looking to put me down, but, sad to say, my response was not so good. The "polite" version of my given response was: "My sister! I have no intention of baring the shame of my nakedness to all and sundry! You must be joking!" (I think if I put my actual response, the book would be x-rated!),

Yet, DeeDee was right, for there came a time in my life when I realized hey, I HAD moved on! I was no longer where I used to be! I'd grown up and was comfortable with being that elusive, mysterious person—ME!

At my current place of fellowship, there's a song that, whenever I hear it, moves me to the core of my being:

> *"Look what Jesus did when He washed me, washed me!*
> *Look what Jesus did when He washed me in the Blood!*
> *Look what Jesus did when He washed me, washed me,*
> *Look what Jesus did when He washed me in the Blood!"*

> And then the chorus says (and I love this bit!):
> *"I'm changed and I know that I am!*
> *I'm changed! And I that I am! "*
> *I'm changed and I know that I am!*
> *I know, I know, I know!!"*

I could never have made it this far without God's help. His hand has literally kept me from sinking and has held my head above the water. In an ancient book it says that "underneath are the everlasting arms" and I have found that to be true in all of my journey circumstances and situations.

During those times when my self-esteem was practically non-existent, even though I'd try to dress and look like a million dollars, He knew my true state of mind and self-opinion. When my emotional mindset was like a washed-out, dingy rag due to life's choices and circumstances, even then God still had me on His mind and was working out *His* plans to move me from my gutter to His glory. In retrospect, He never left me nor forsook me, even though I often felt He either didn't care or was punishing me for what I had done. And yes, there were many times when I doubted His existence, but that same ancient book says that "love is stronger than death". Even if you kill the perception of a person, you can never kill the reality—and so it was with God. I may have doubted

His existence, but the reality of His love, His care, His grace and mercy were too strong to ignore.

Now, I can testify to His love, compassion and saving grace. The aim of this little journal is to help sistas along their own path and life journey and I pray this little book will do just that. And remember . . . there is always One Who walks with you.

Final Journey Pause: *I'm sharing the following journal entry of 18/2/2009:*

> *"Listened to T D Jakes today: "Lord, do something I've never seen before!" Now, it was like the Holy Spirit just had me reclining on the sofa to sit and listen. What got to me was the fact the blind man (at the pool of Siloam) was "created" for God's glory, and Jesus said as much when asked who's sin had initially caused the man's blindness. The blind man never imagined he could ever see—but God did! When He created him, He programmed in a "deliverance day" so that God would get all the glory!*
>
> *And that was the issue I was chewing over on my way home; that my life seemed of little / no consequence; that despite my many, many, MANY soul ties (including international ones!) I remembered Tunisia yesterday (have mercy) and others . . . but I recognize my life is a divine set up designed for God to get all the glory.*
>
> *So . . . I maybe illegitimate, financially challenged, no car, cracked house, rude boss (he called me a bloody idiot today, for real!); I might be in a dead-end job, no relationship, no man, no husband, no children, overweight and underpaid, etc, etc, etc—God is about to do SOMETHING I've never seen before! What an amazing and liberating thought. After so many relationships, God is STILL in control.*

My sista, I'm sharing the above journal entry written shortly after my "Pandora Box" experience to encourage you. When you think you're path is just a dead-end, just be still, take a deep breath. Yes, do it right now, right where you are. Fill your lungs with hope and promises of a better tomorrow and breathe out the carbon dioxide of yesterday.

You have come this far and even holding his book is a part of your journey. Know that the One who walked with me, often at those times when I felt alone, unloved, unwanted—also walks with you. He is only a breath, a prayer, a heart sigh away. So why not call Him? That tug on your heart is His hand of love. How do you call Him? Breathe in the air He made—and let Him in. God is much nearer to you than you could ever imagine.

Sista, you don't have to walk the rest of your journey alone, ever . . . not when there's One who walks with you, even now, is ever by your side . . . . Call Him. Take His hand. Your journey will never be the same. Yep, it's time to get back up again . . . your journey is just beginning . . . .

Lightning Source UK Ltd.
Milton Keynes UK
UKOW040119201112

202436UK00001B/80/P